Simple Designs II

DRAWINGS BY KIMBERLY GARVEY

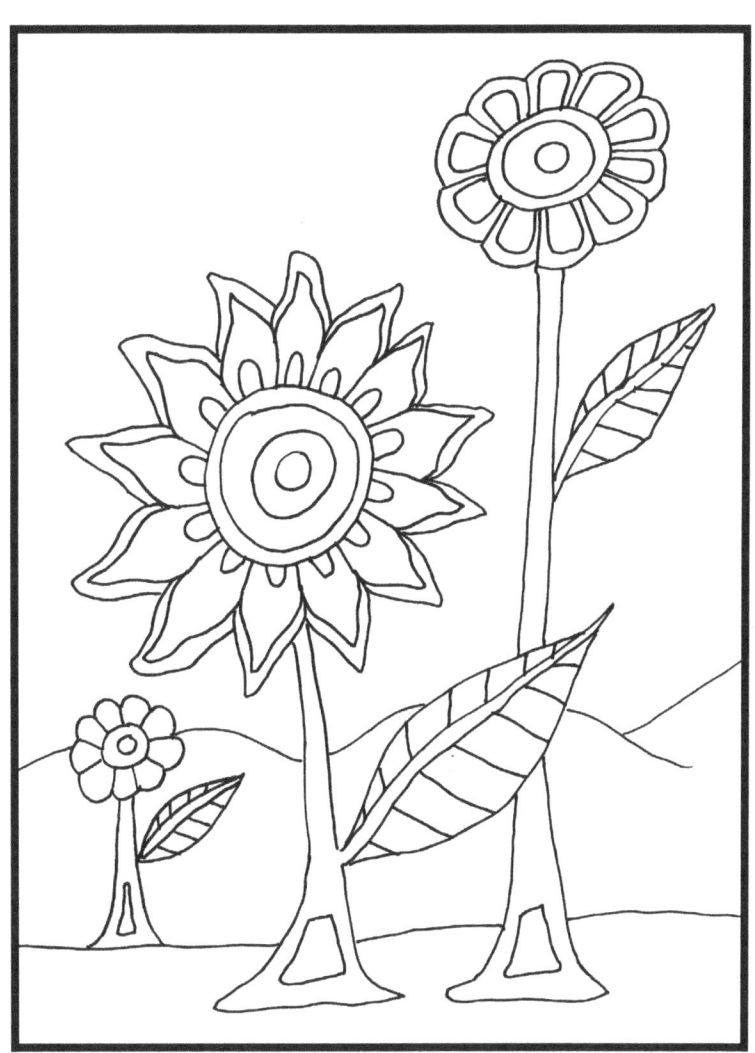

Another Easy Coloring Book for All

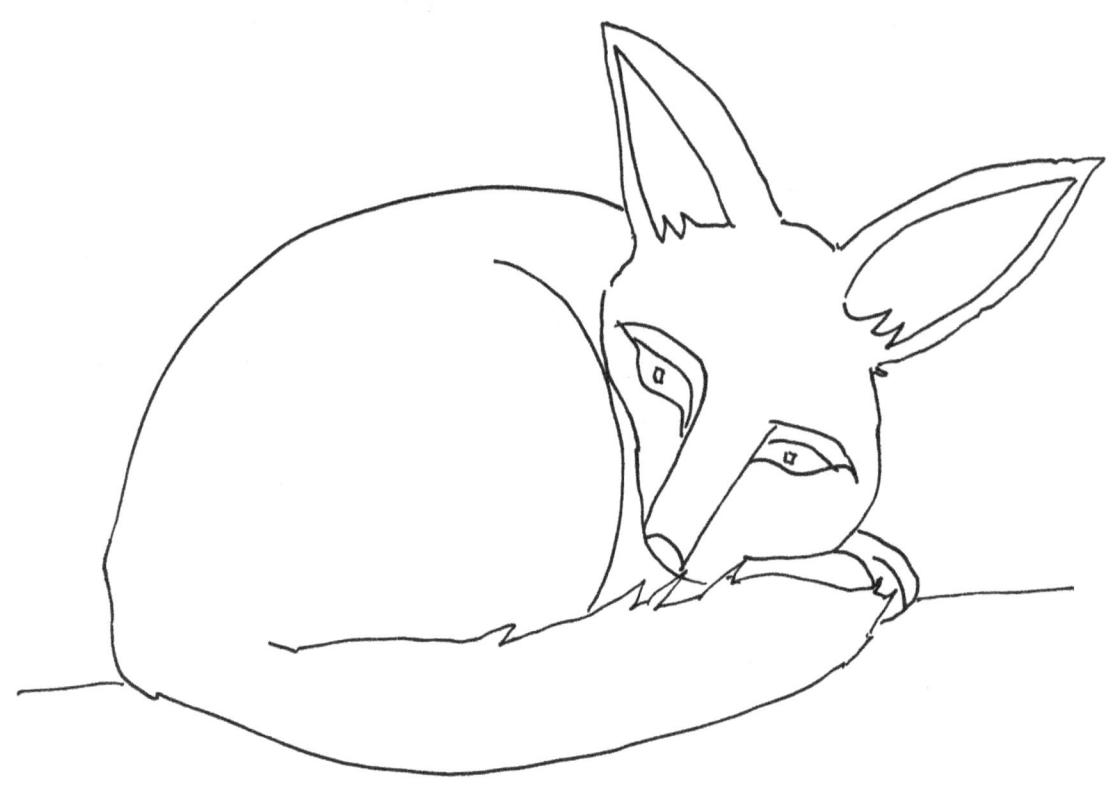

Kimberlygarvey.com

Kimberlygarvey.com

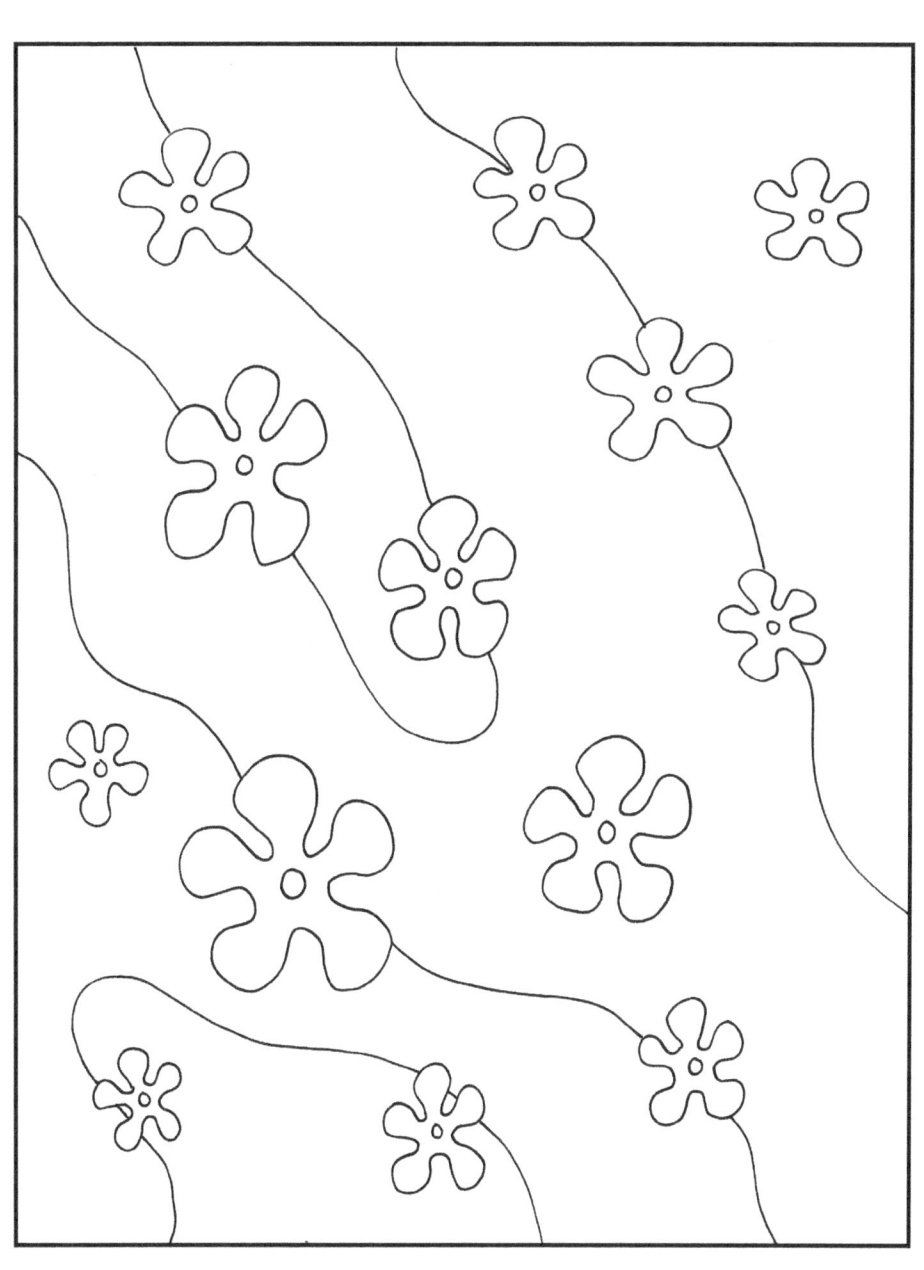

WARNING!!!!

Please put a protection sheet of paper between the pages when using markers to prevent bleed-through.

A protection sheet is included at the back of this book.

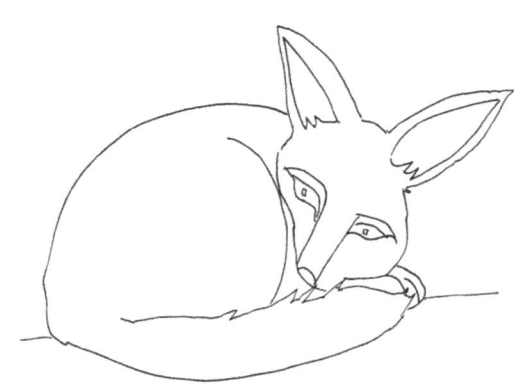

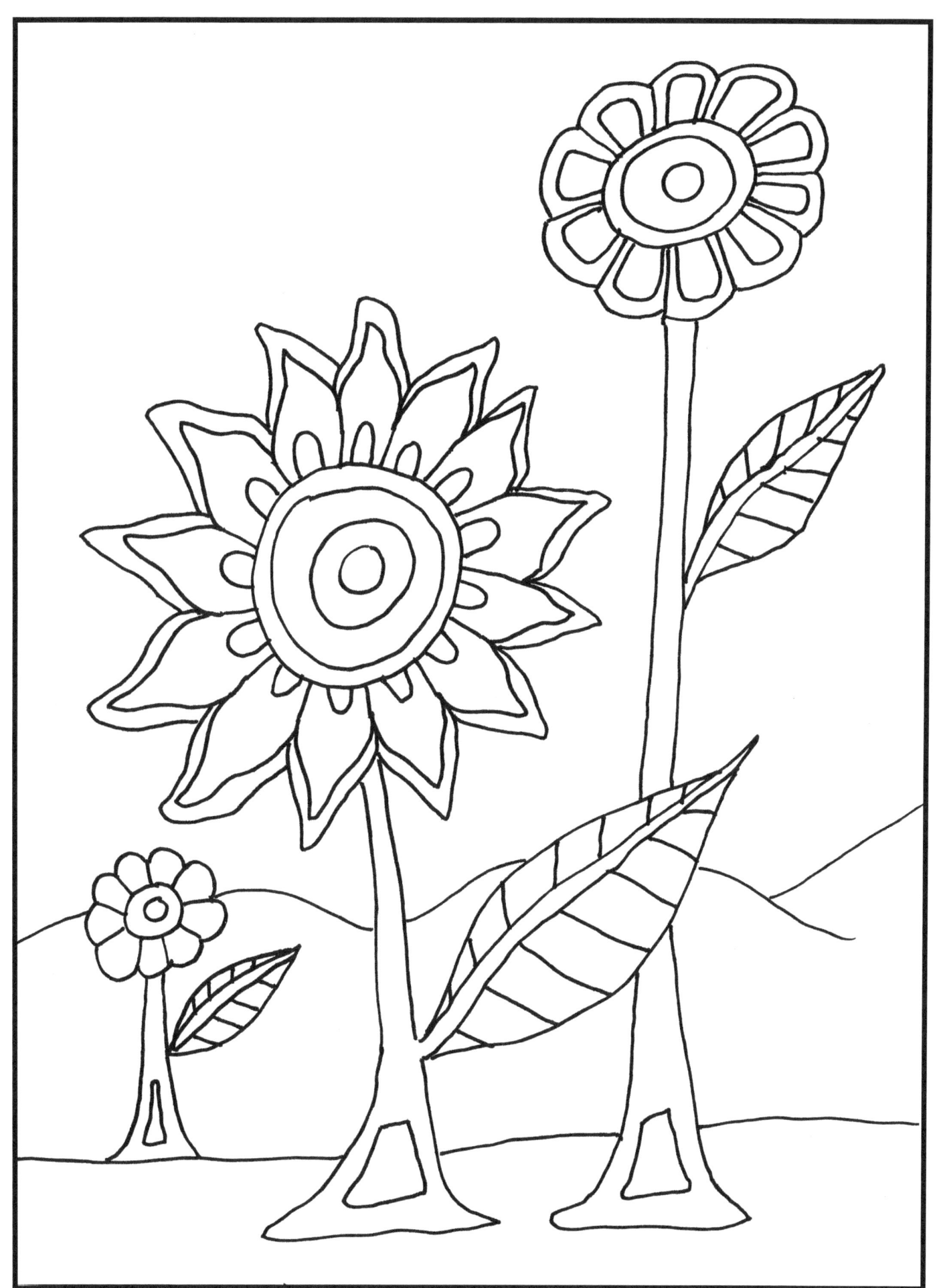

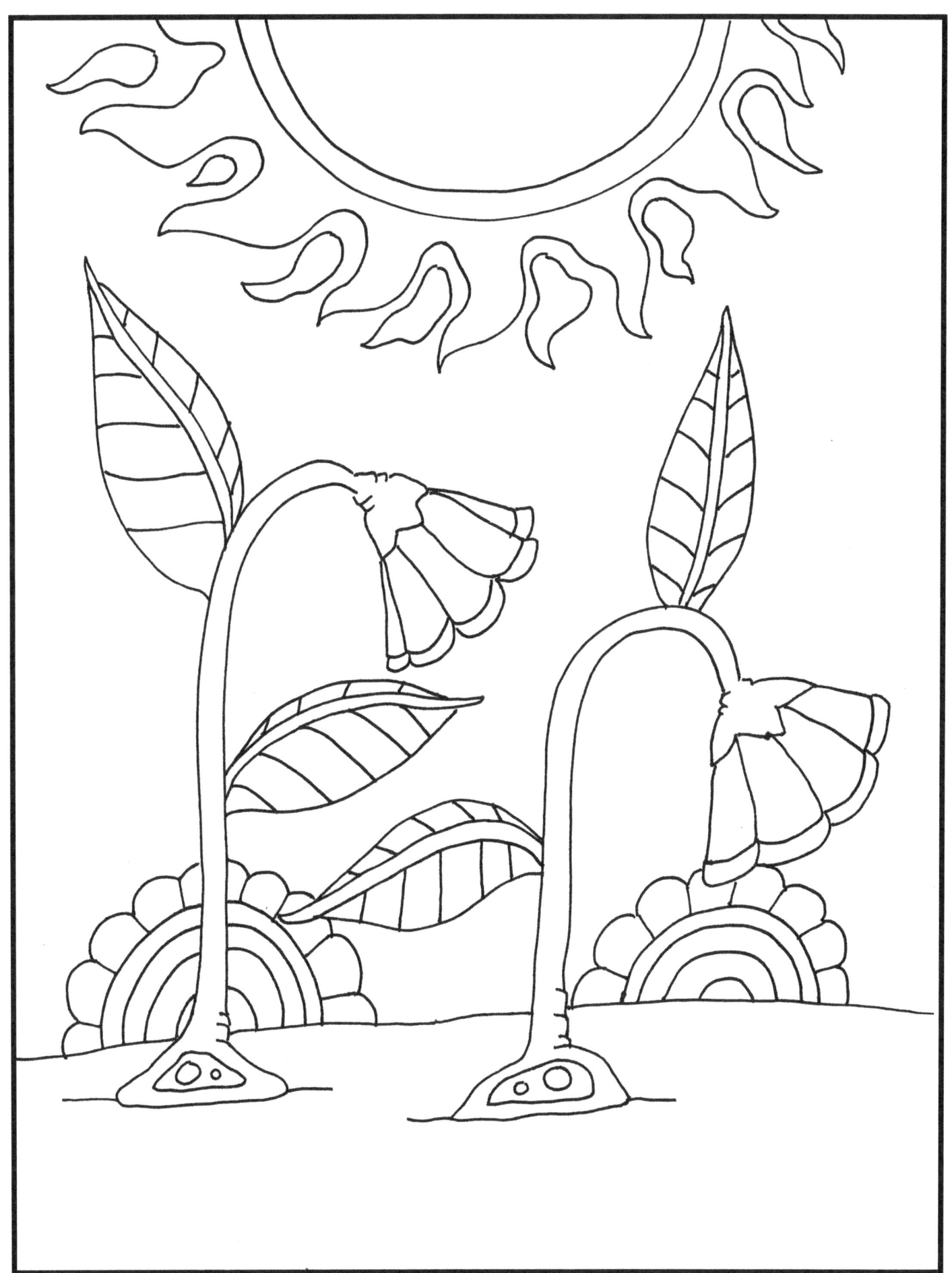

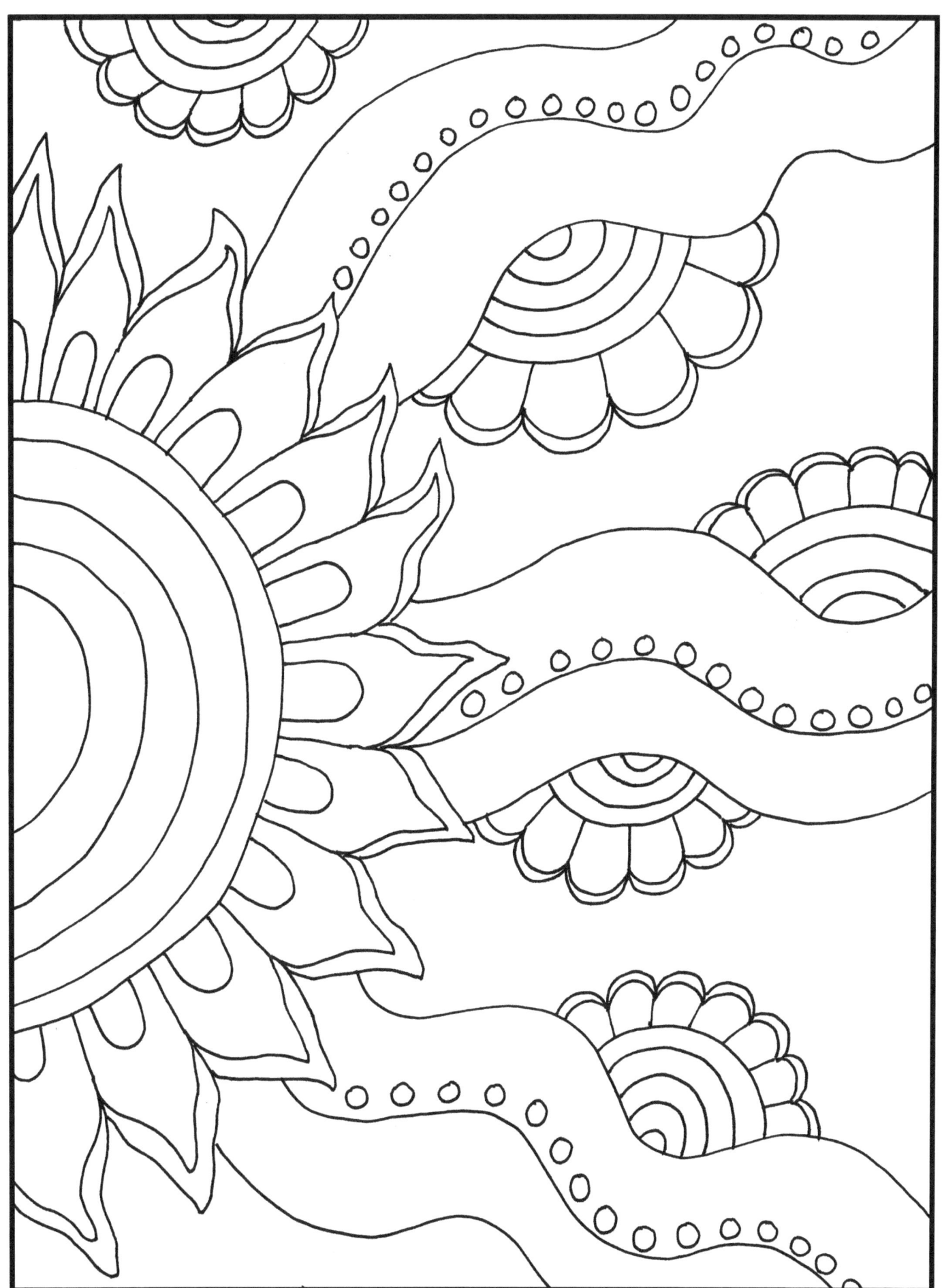

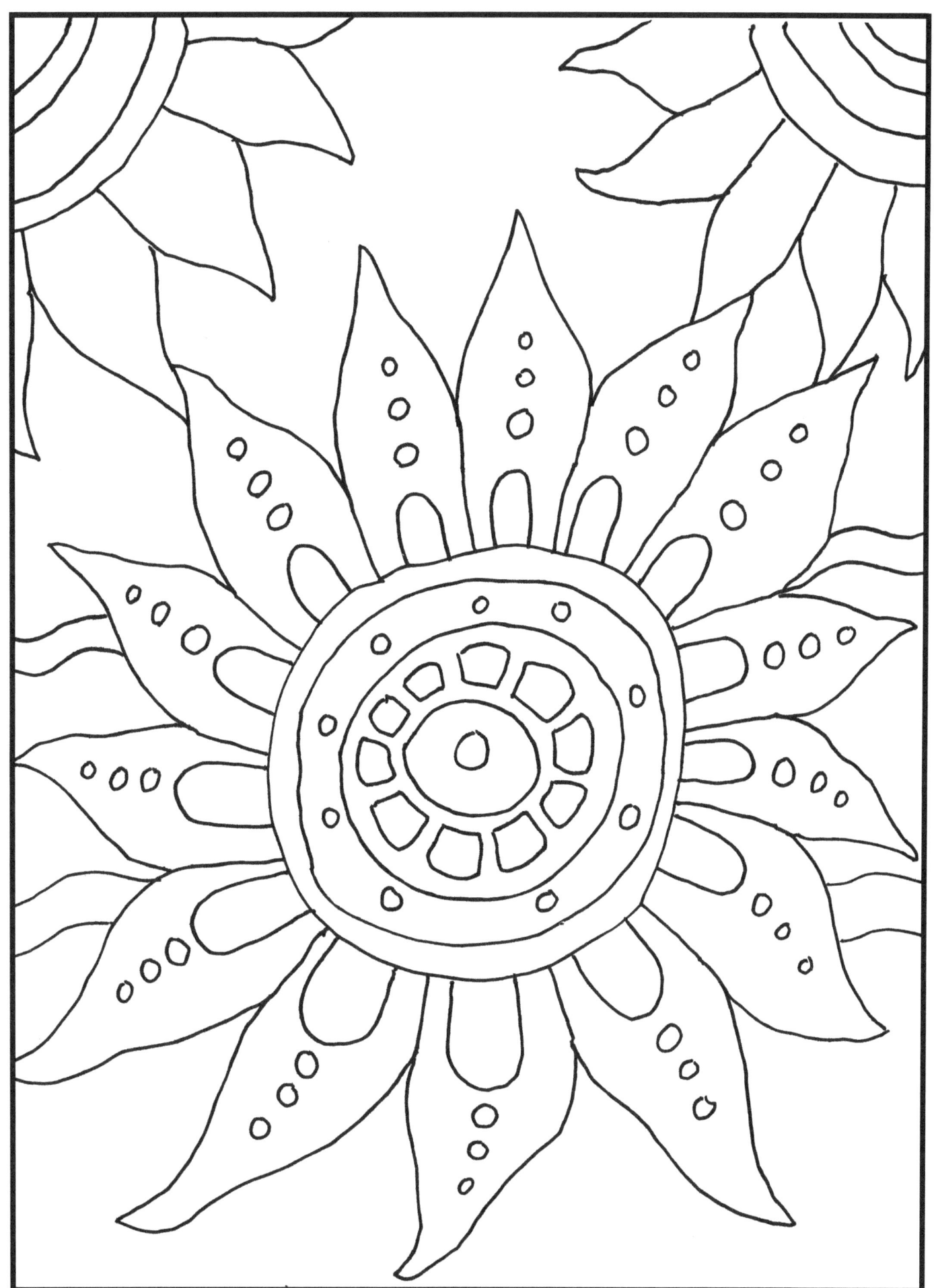

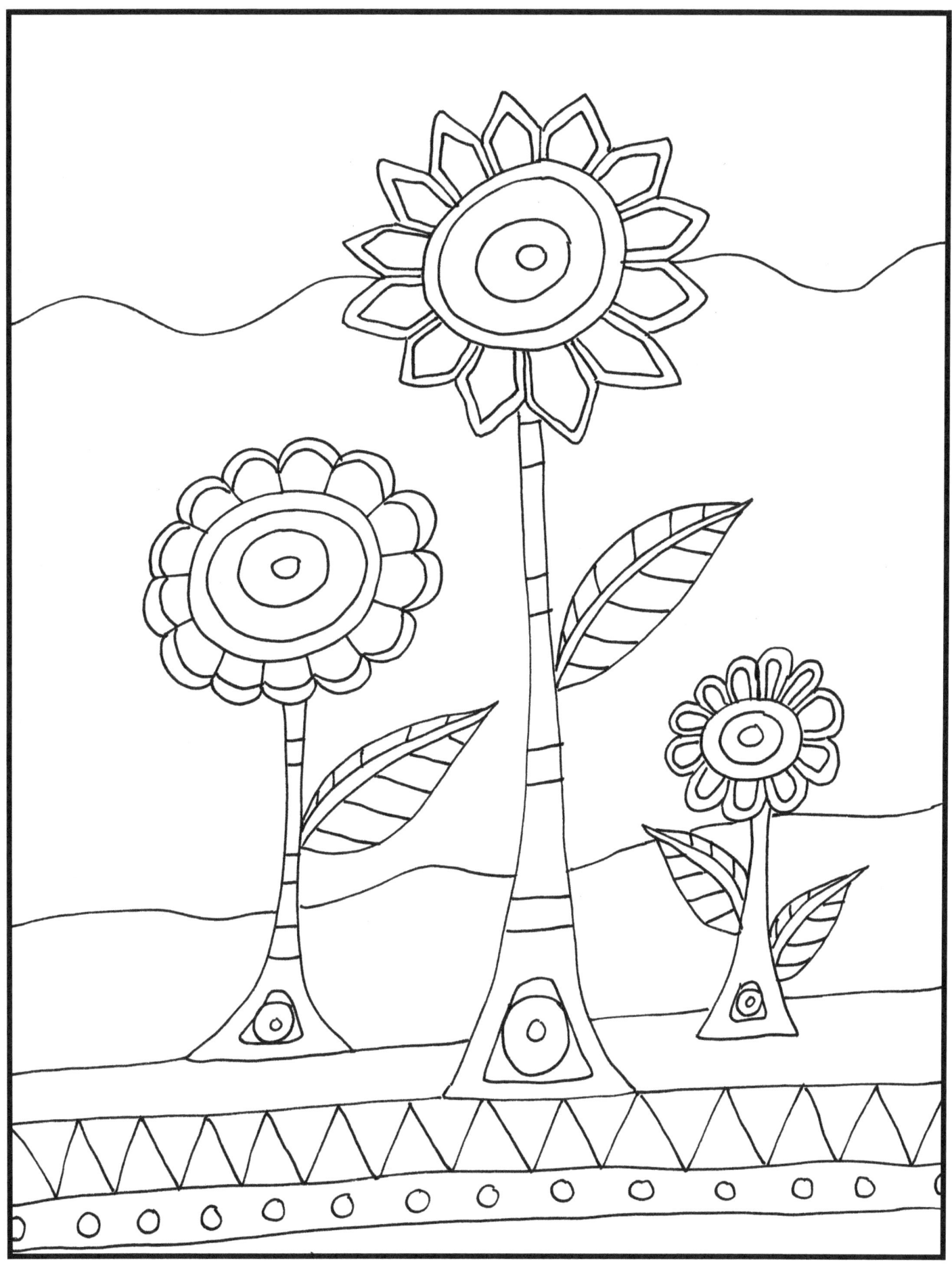

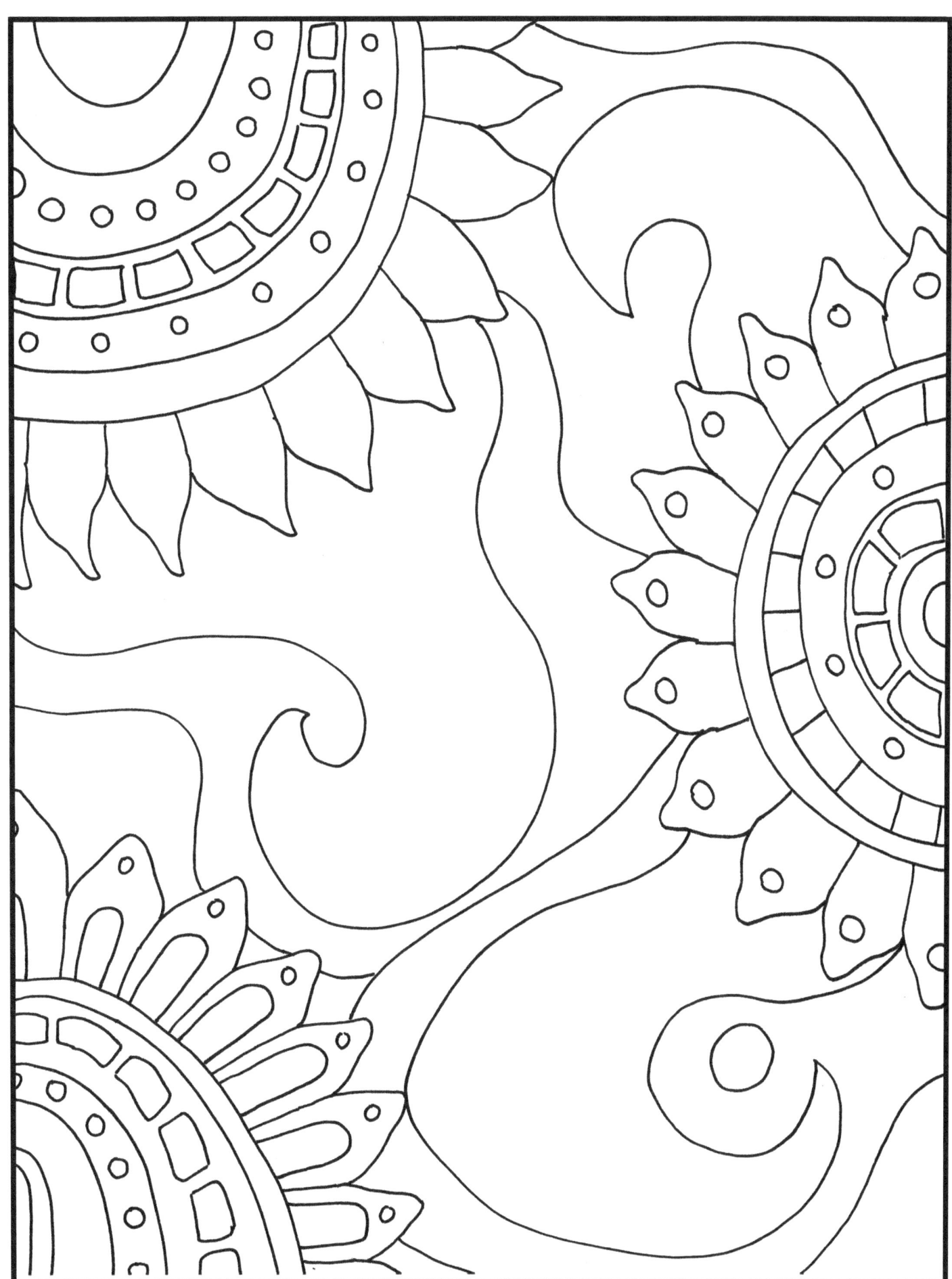

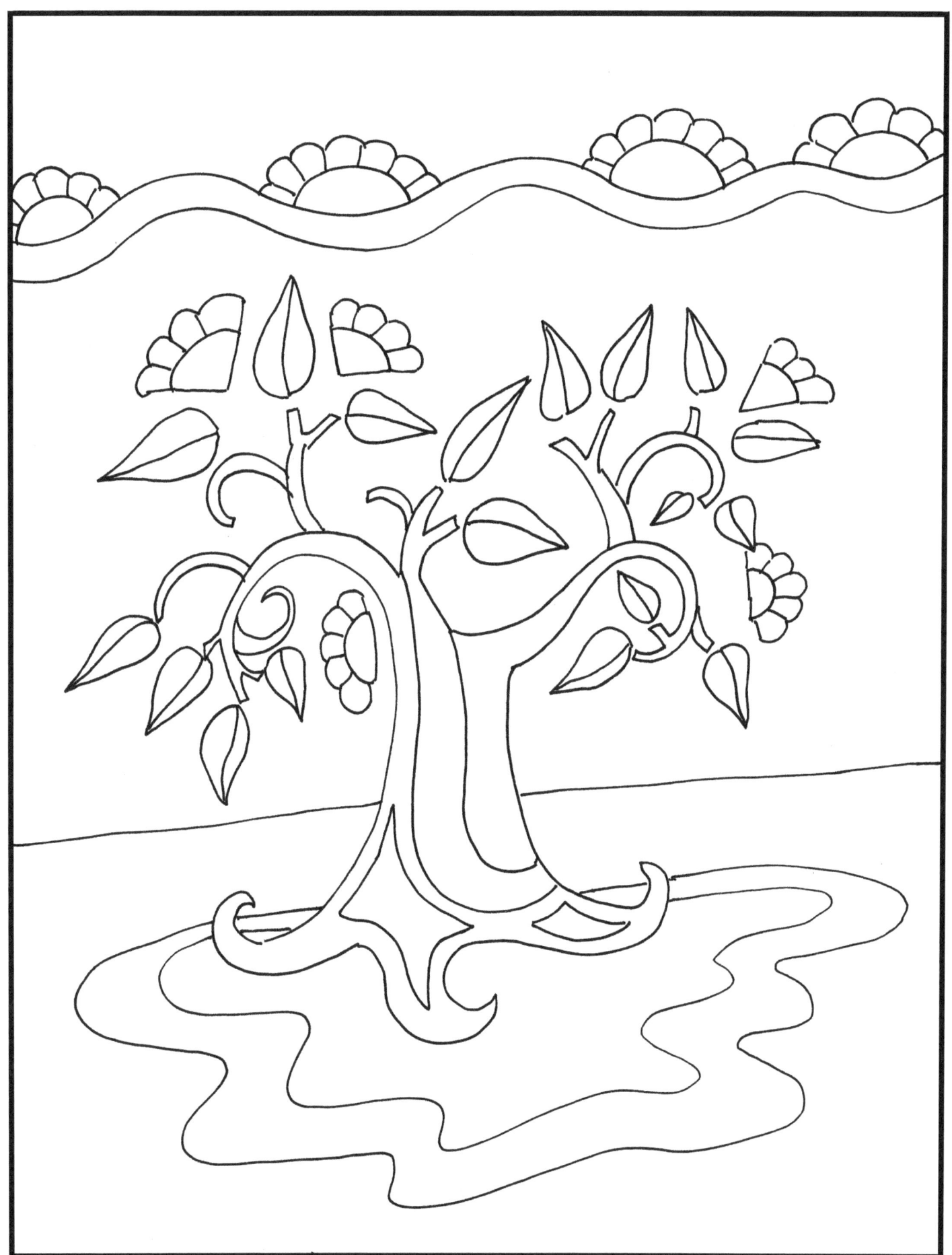

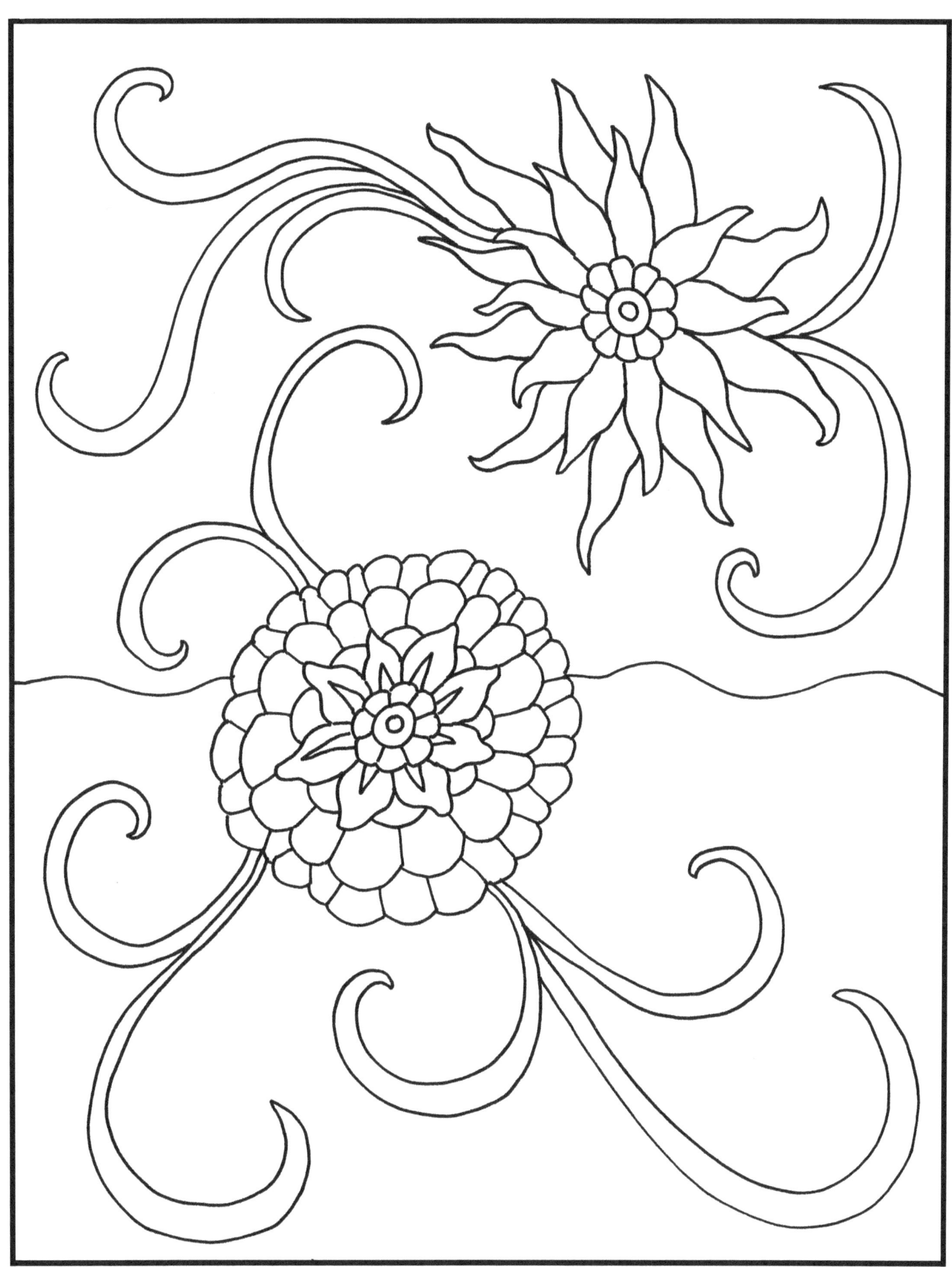

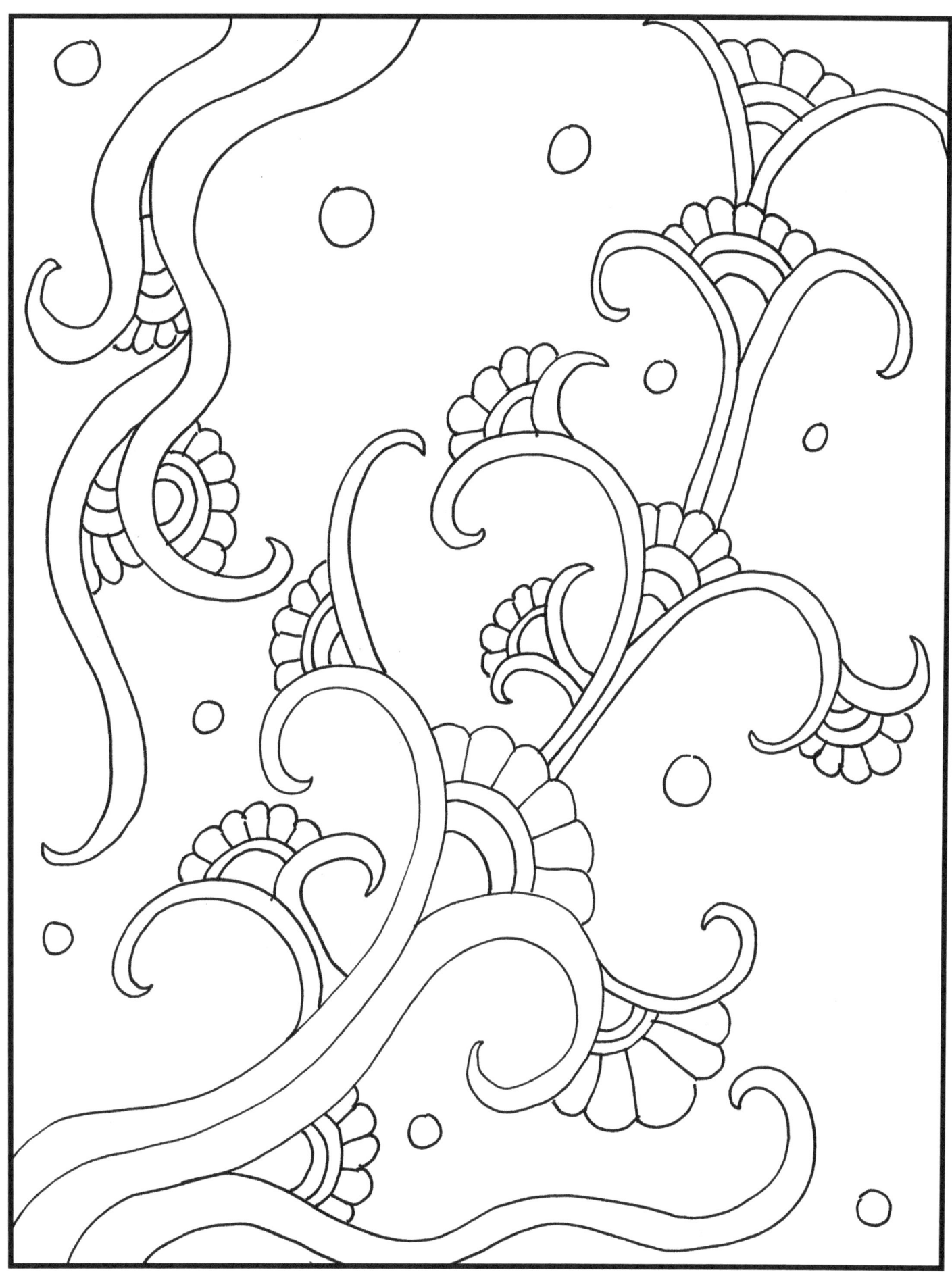

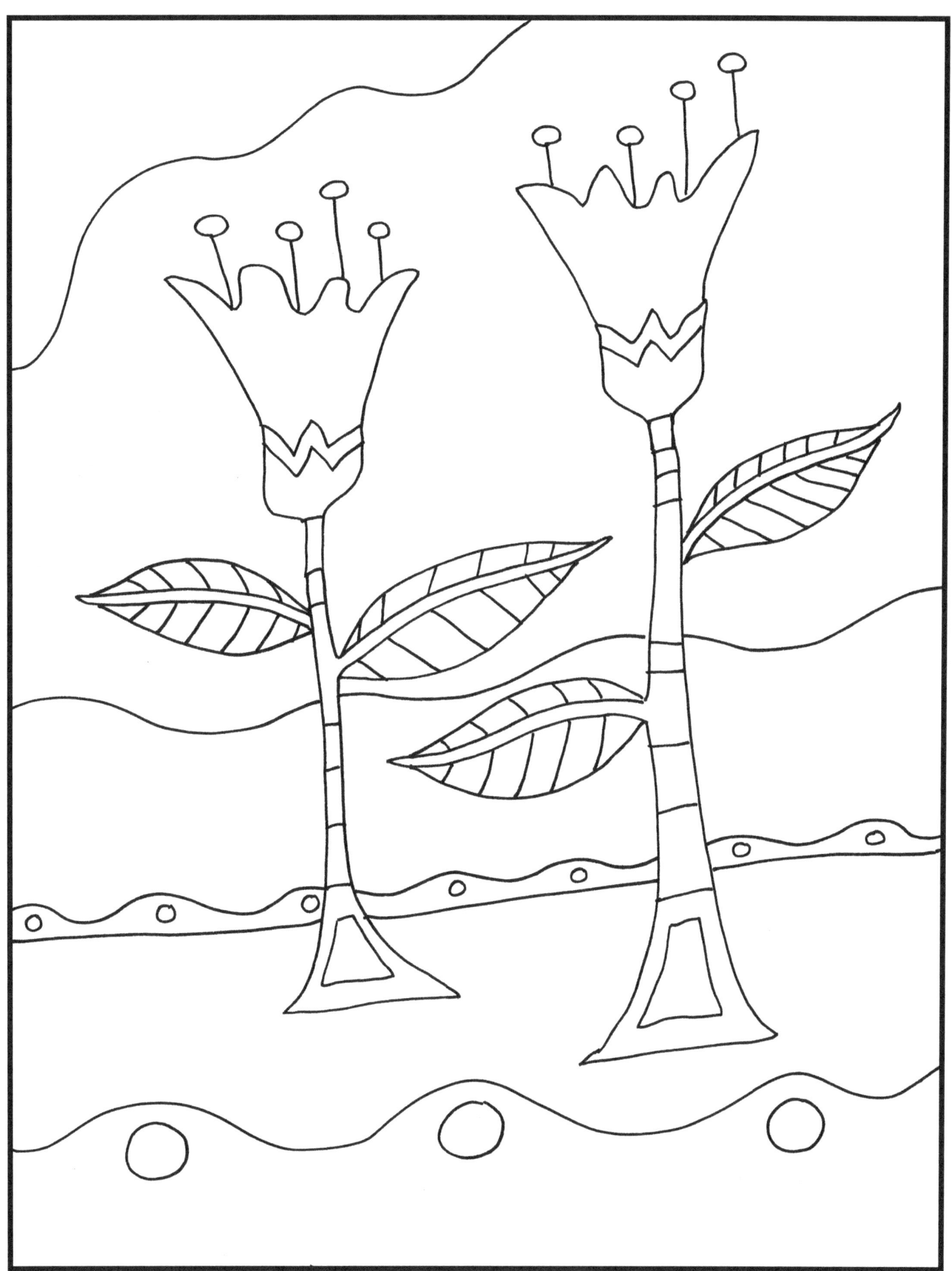

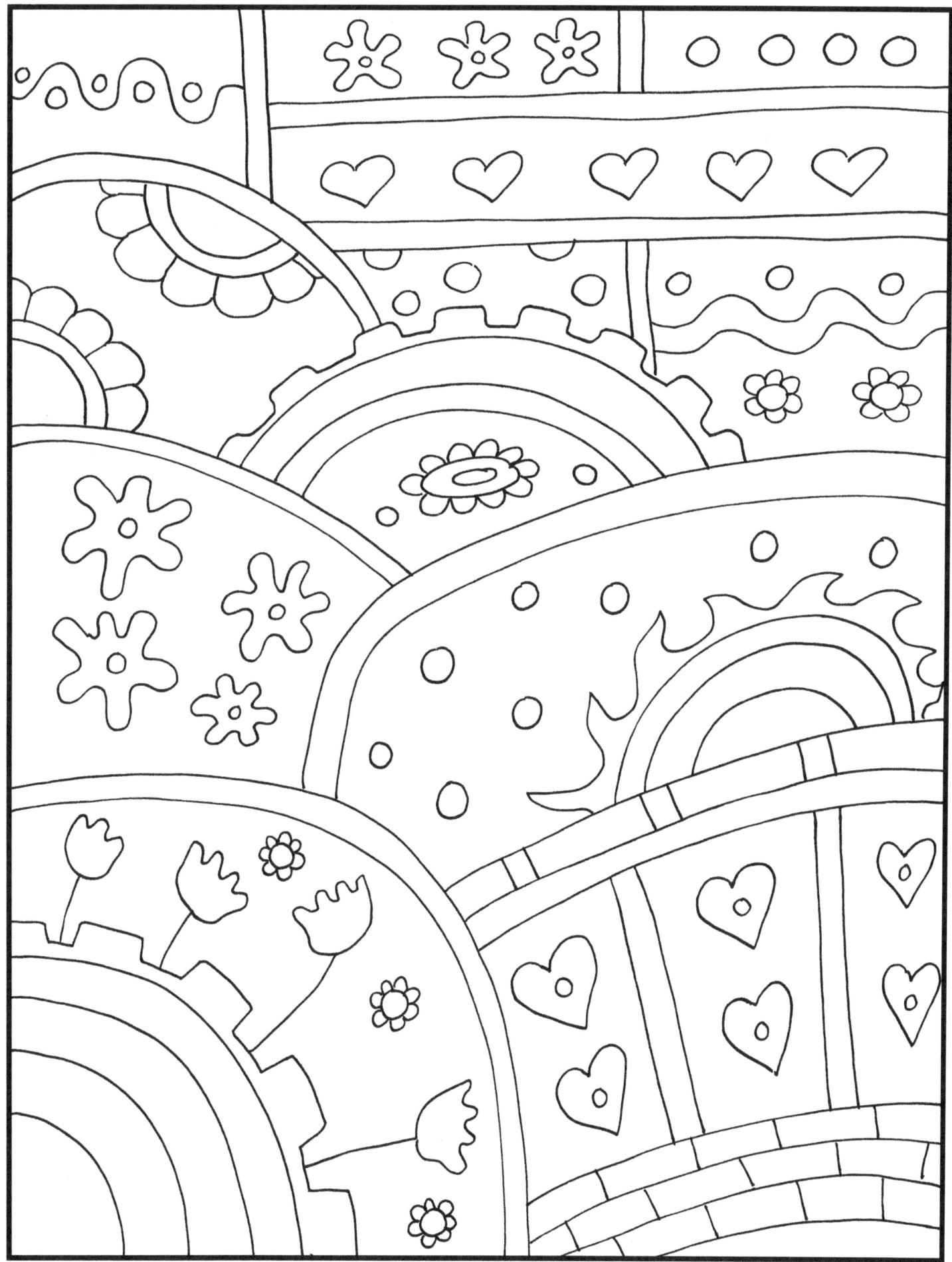

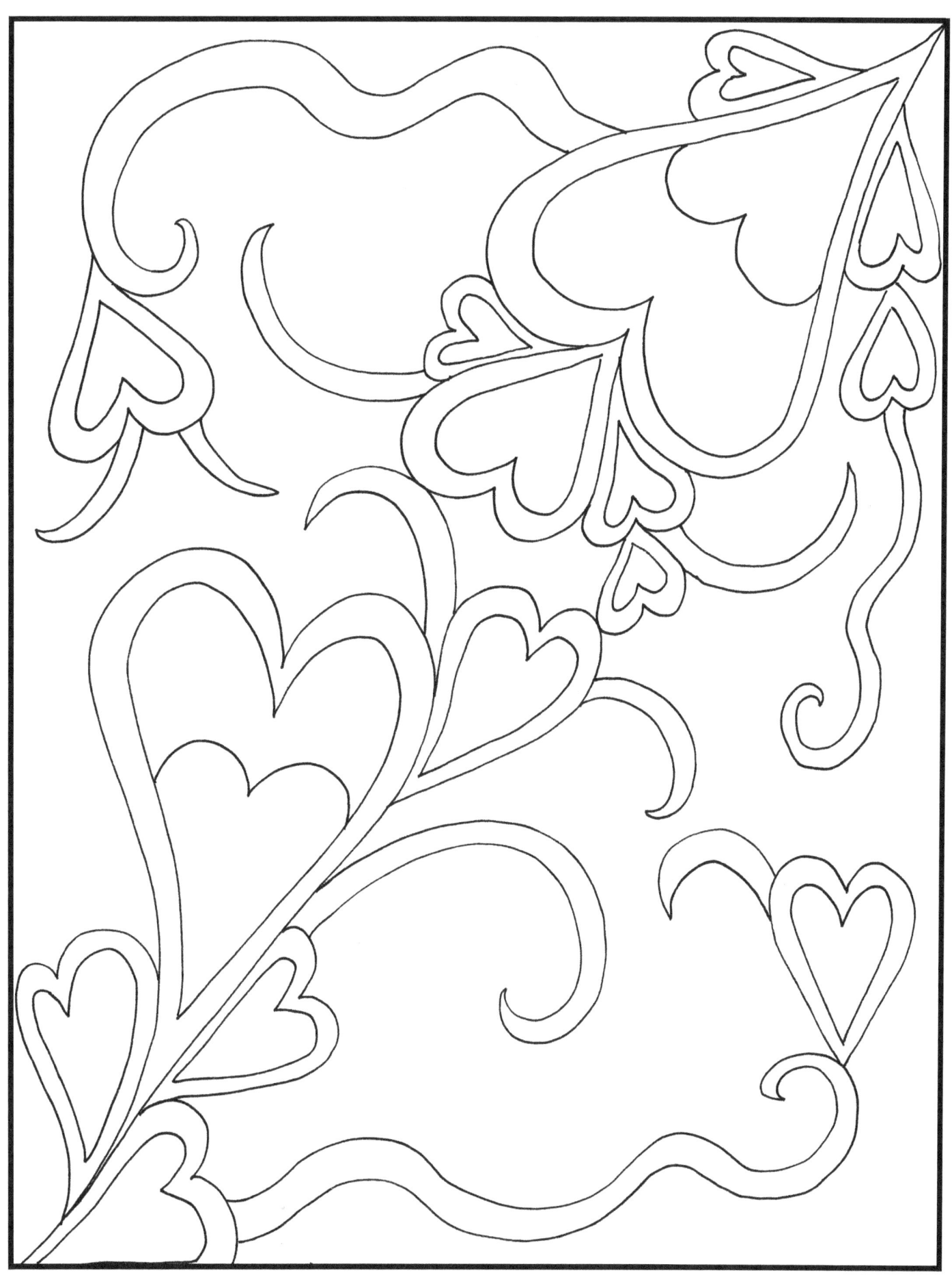

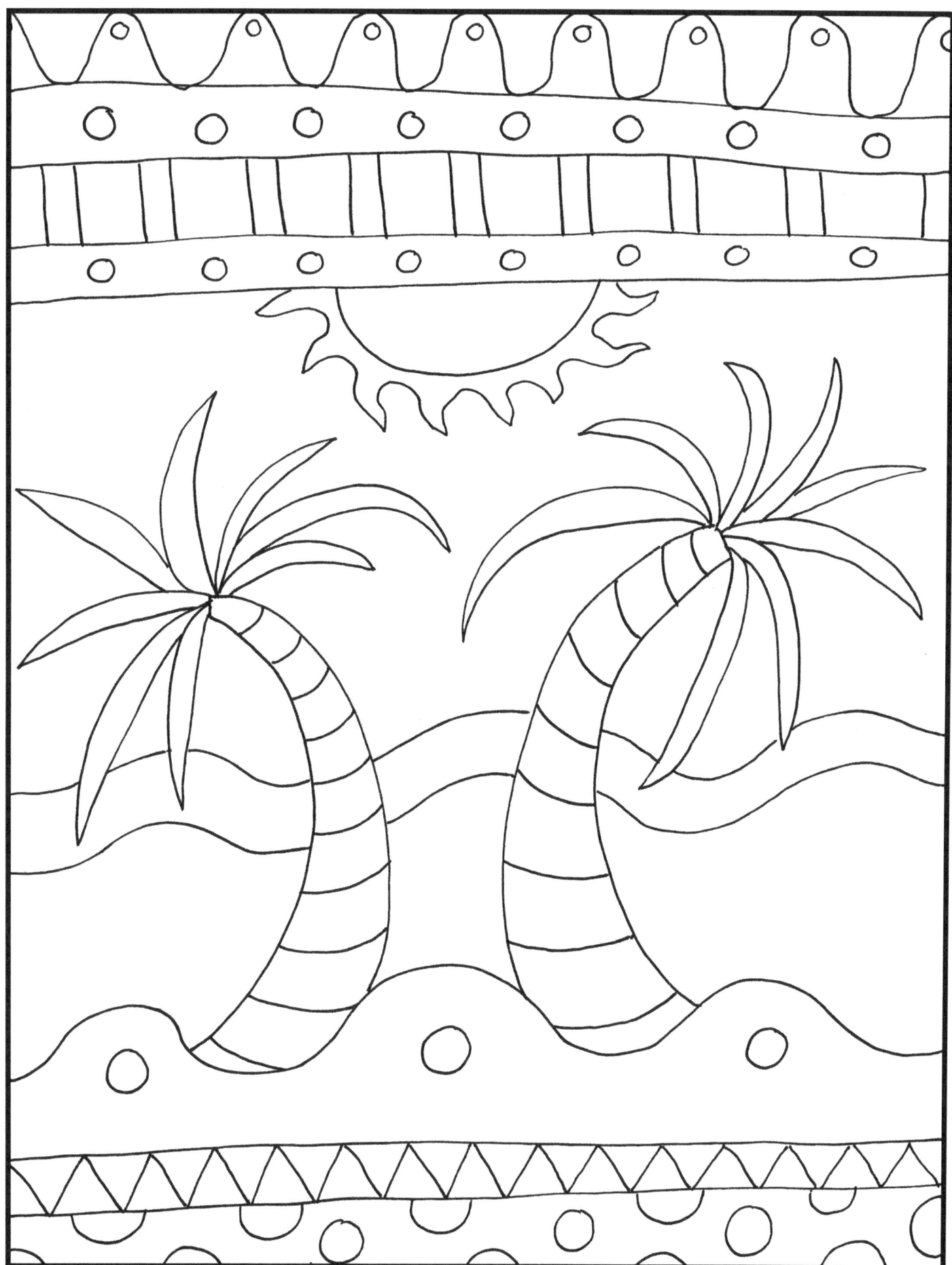

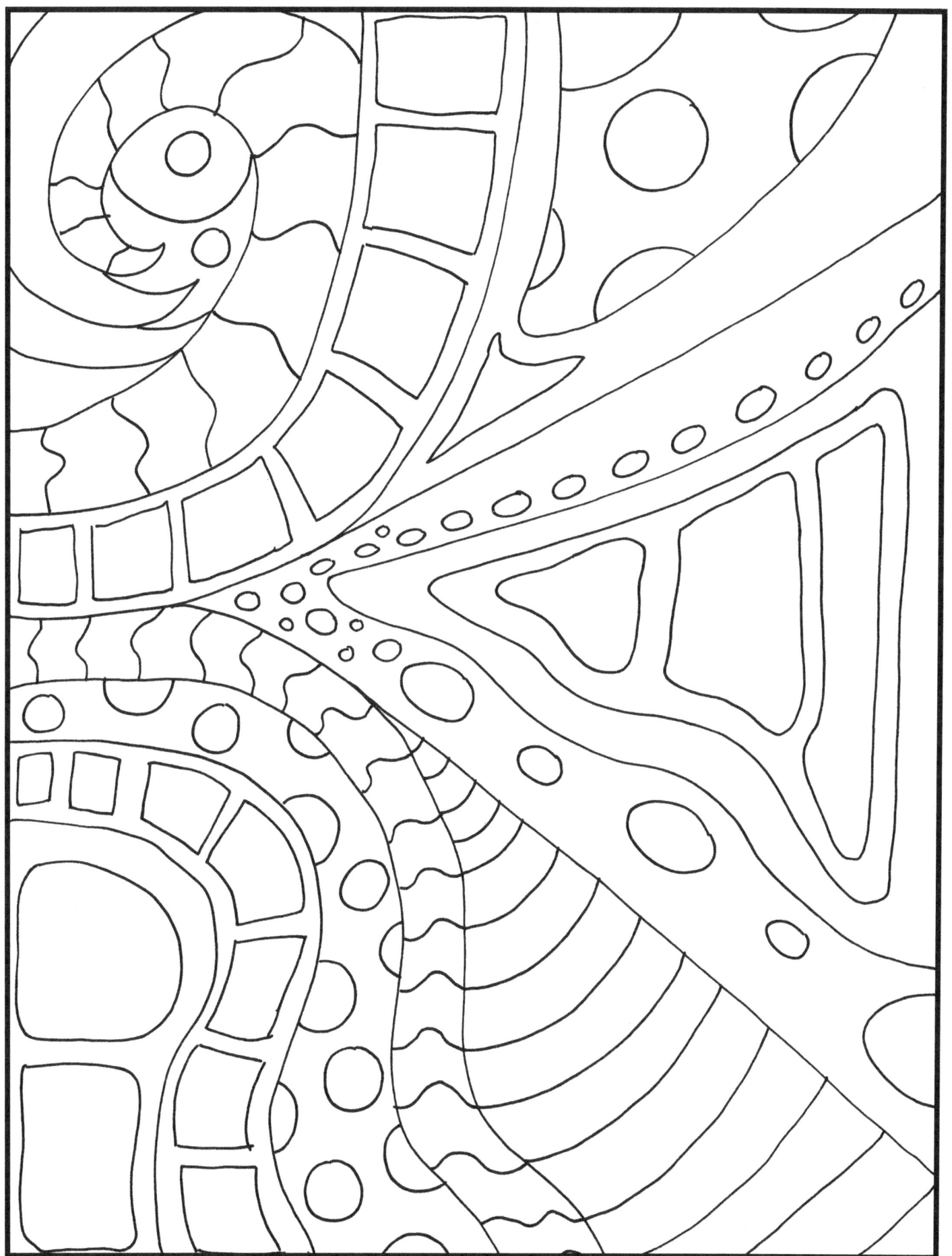

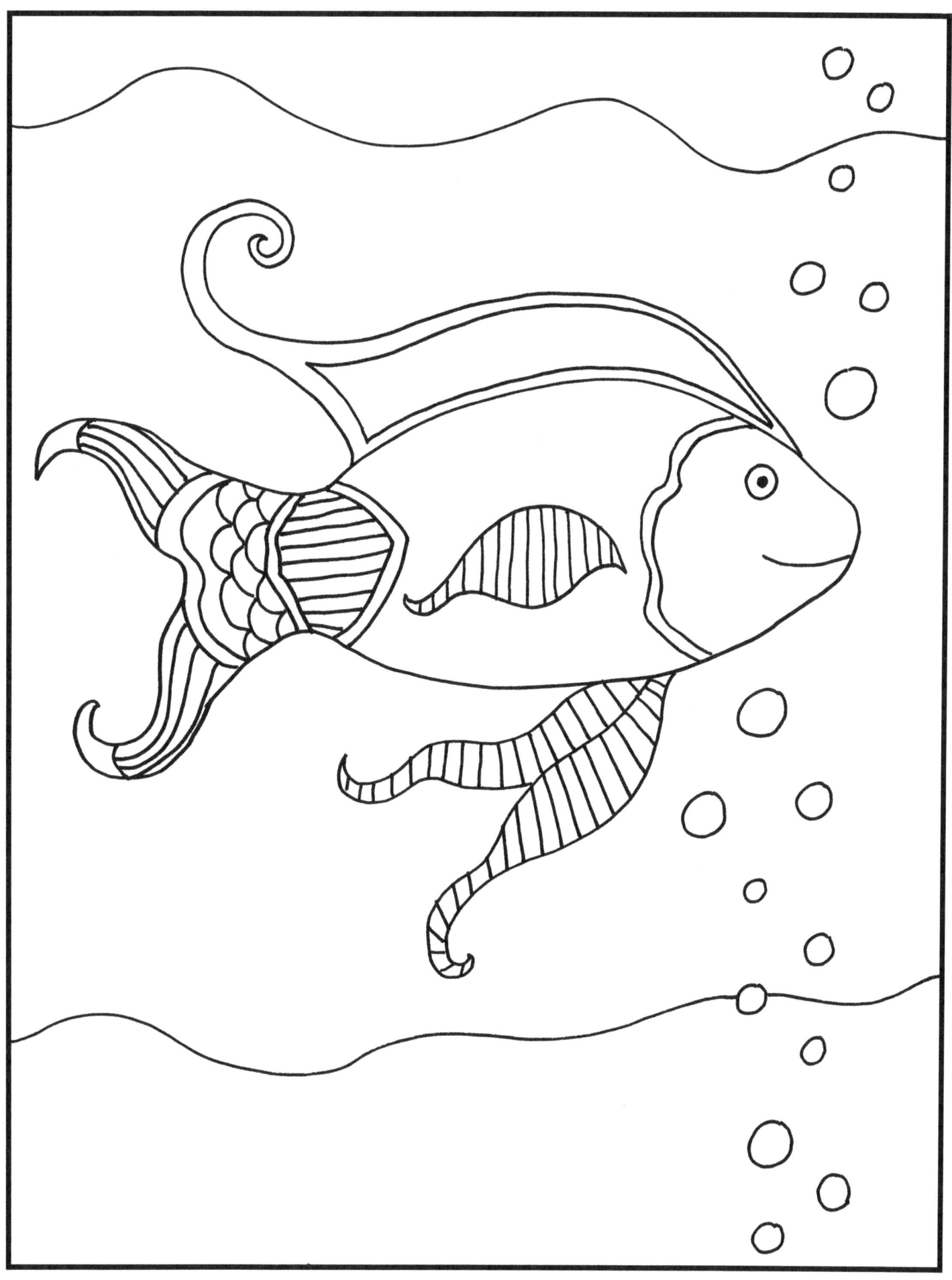

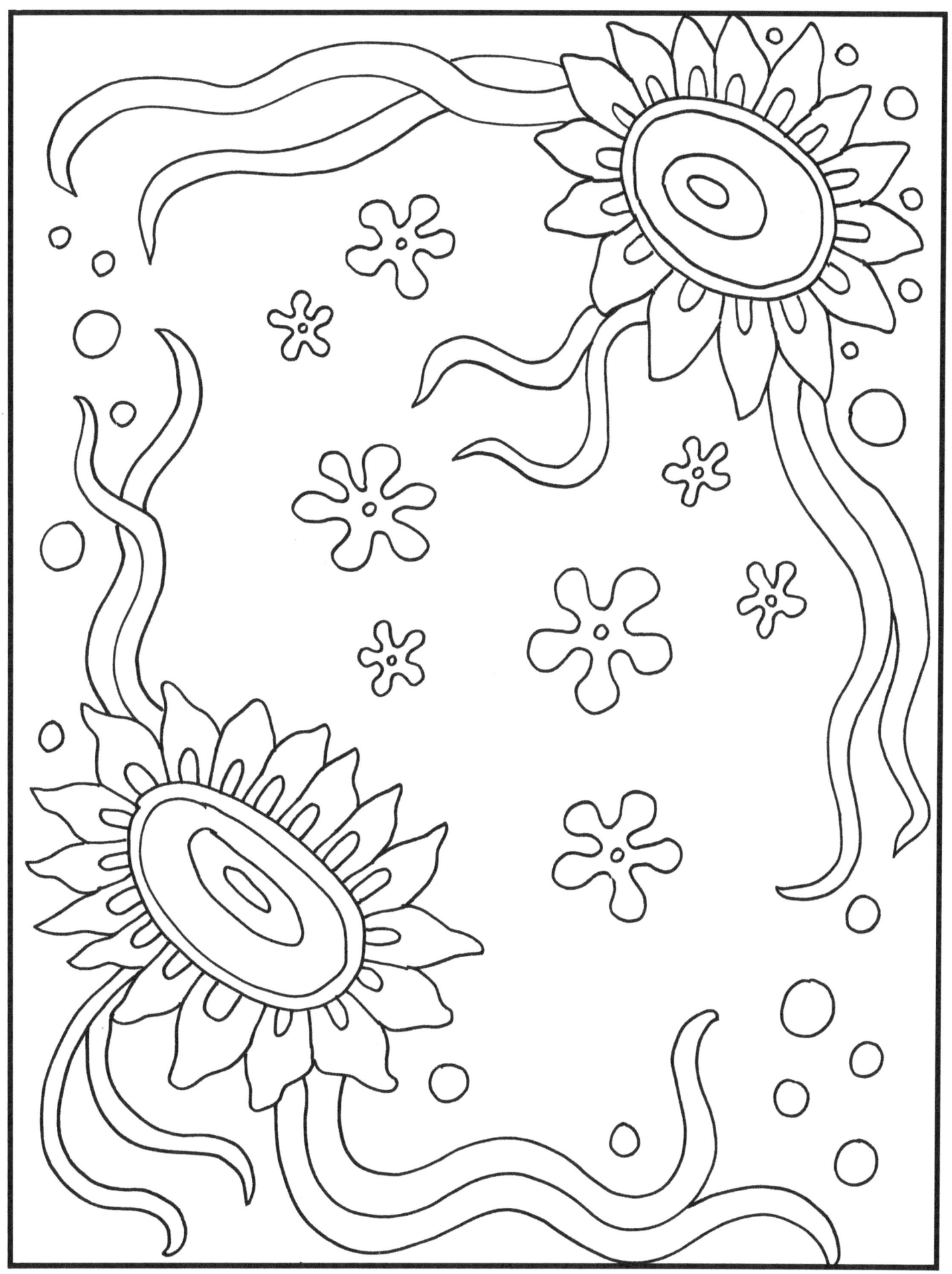

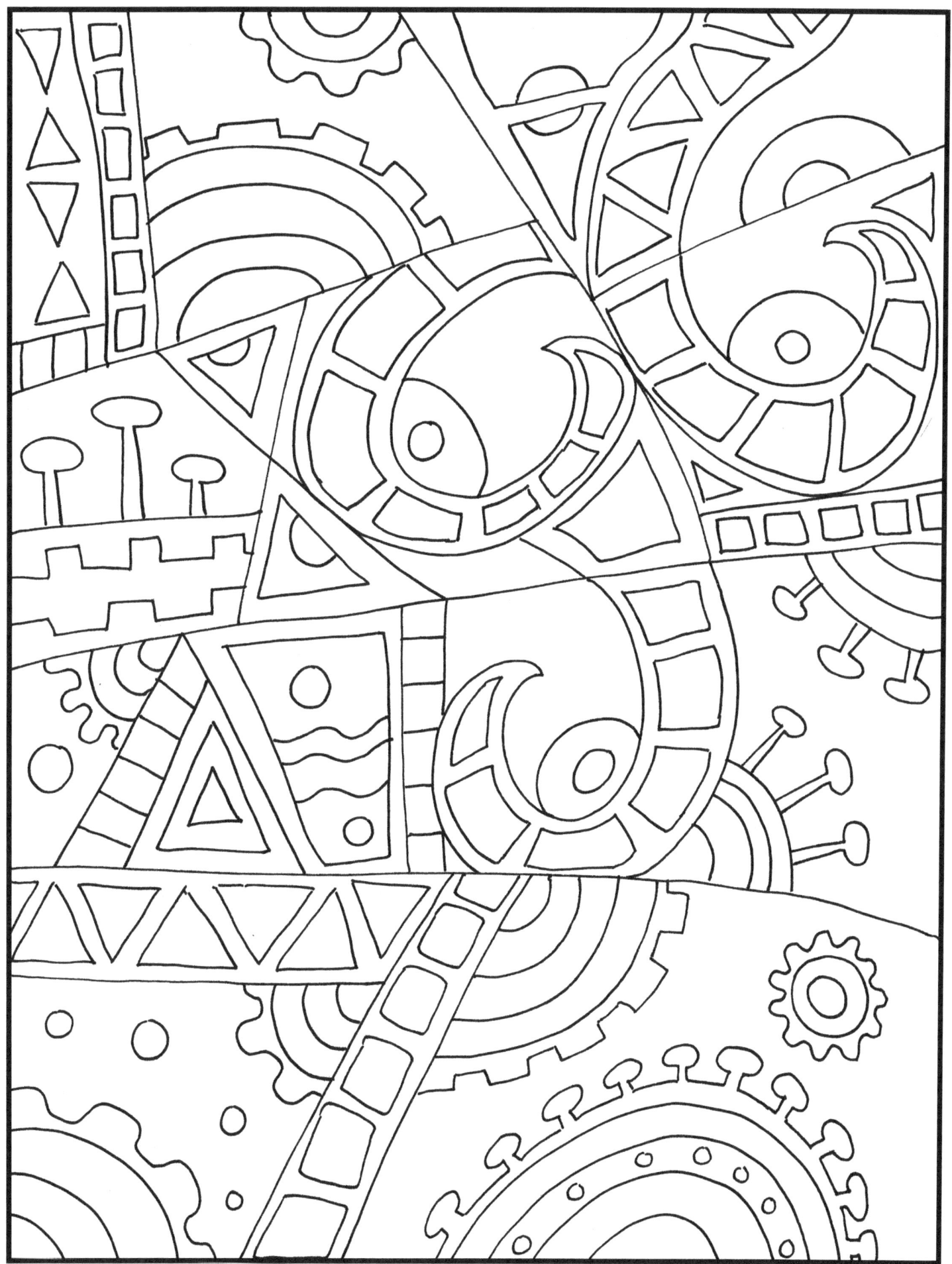

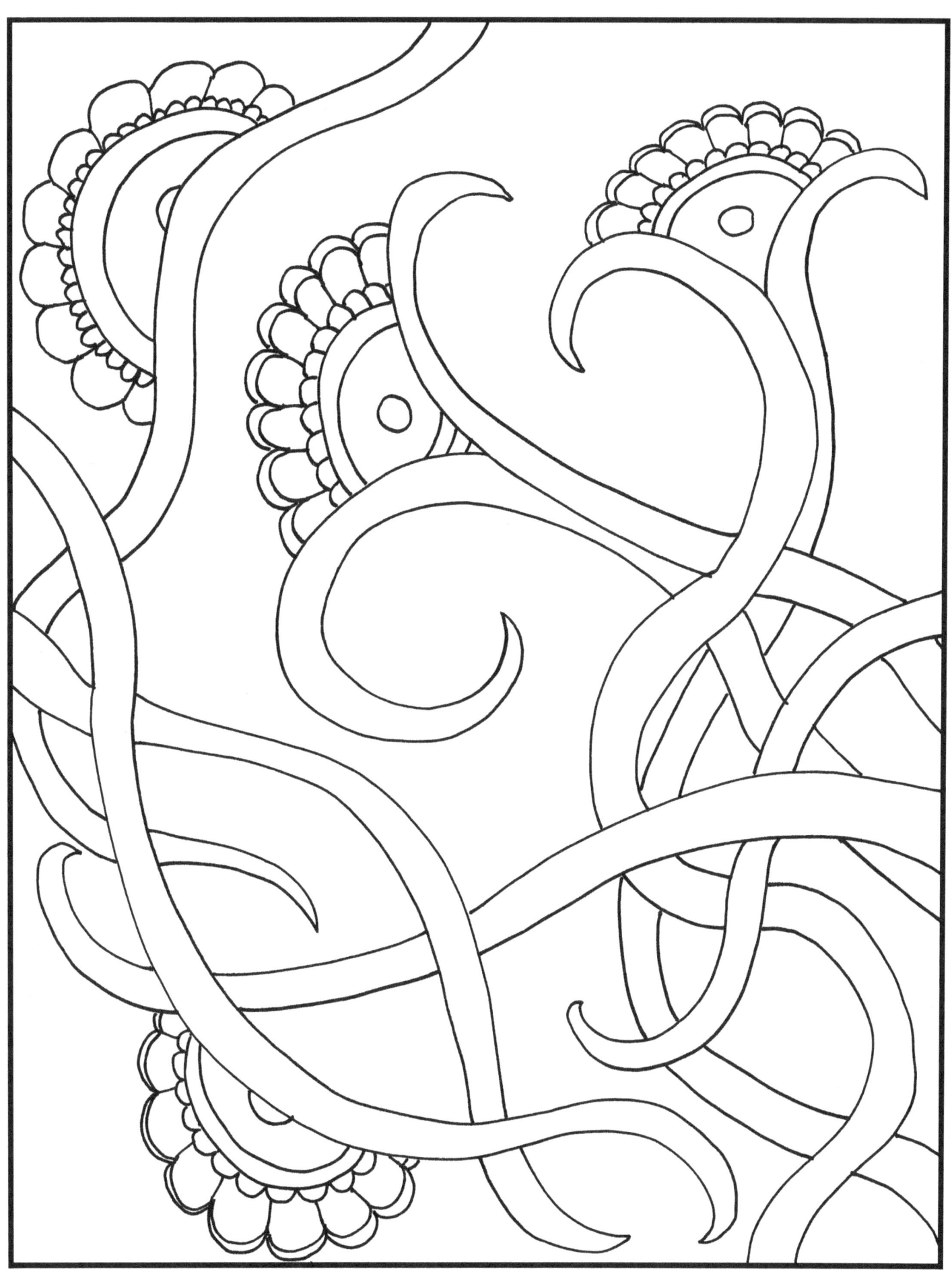

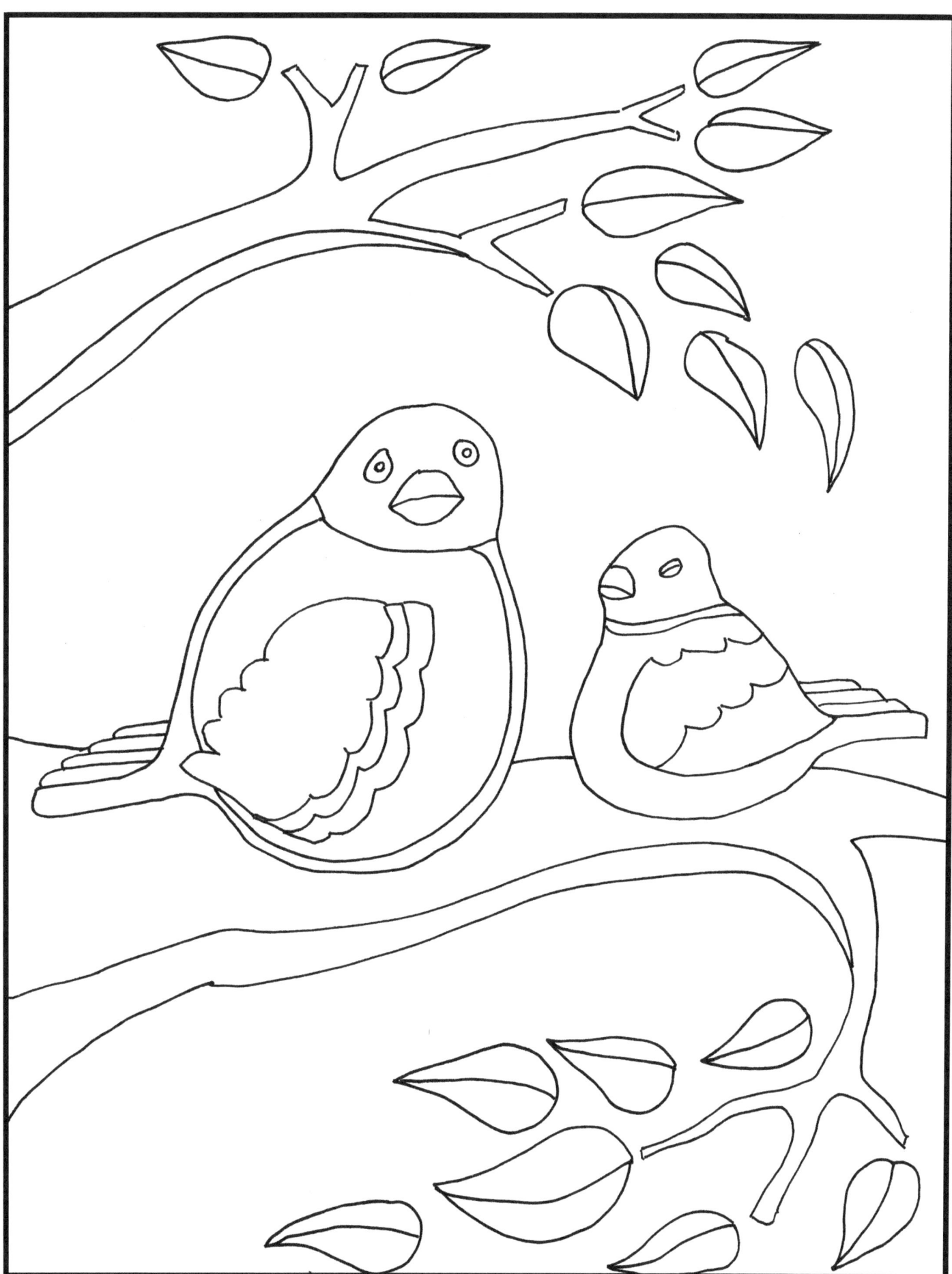

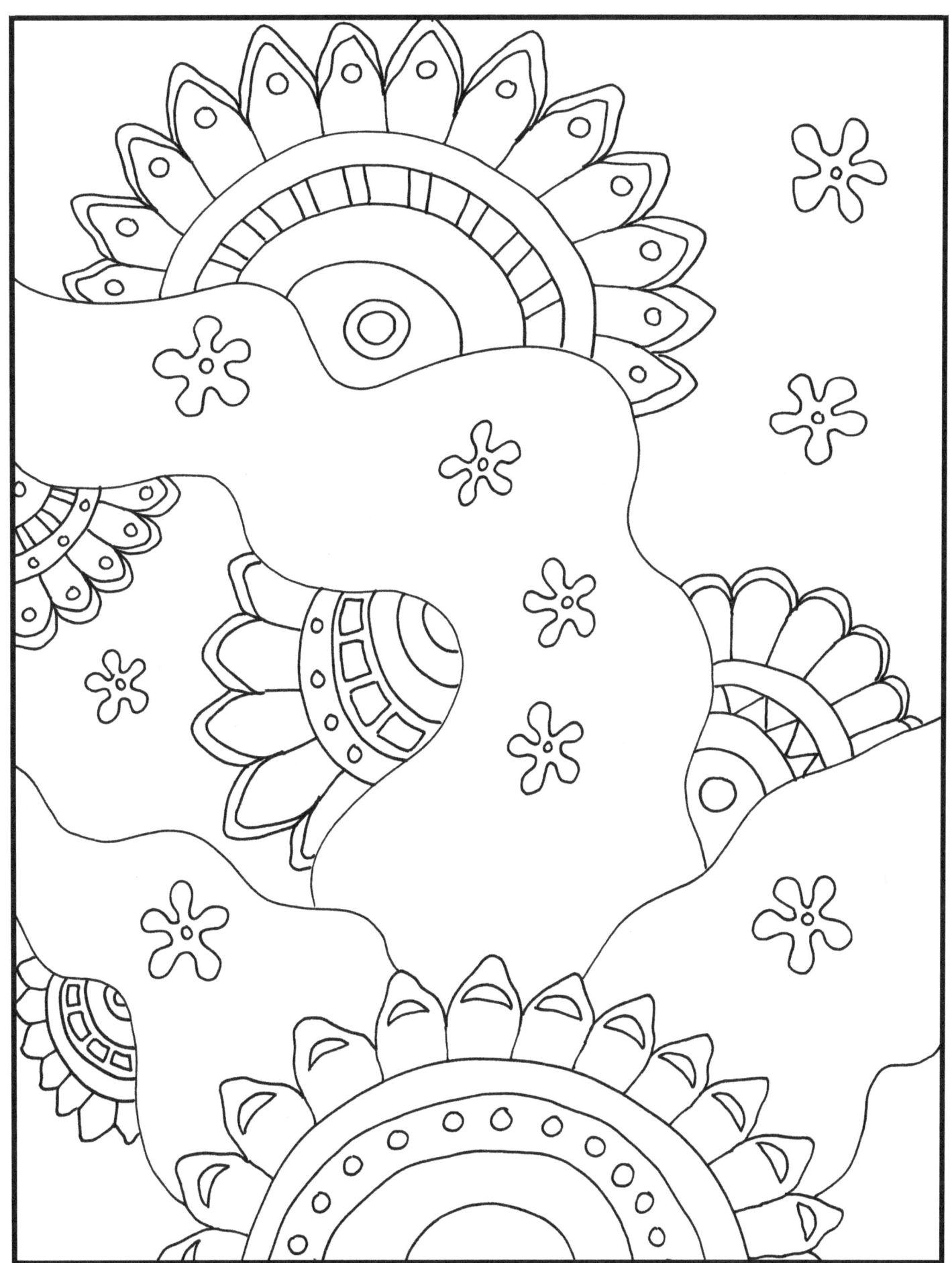

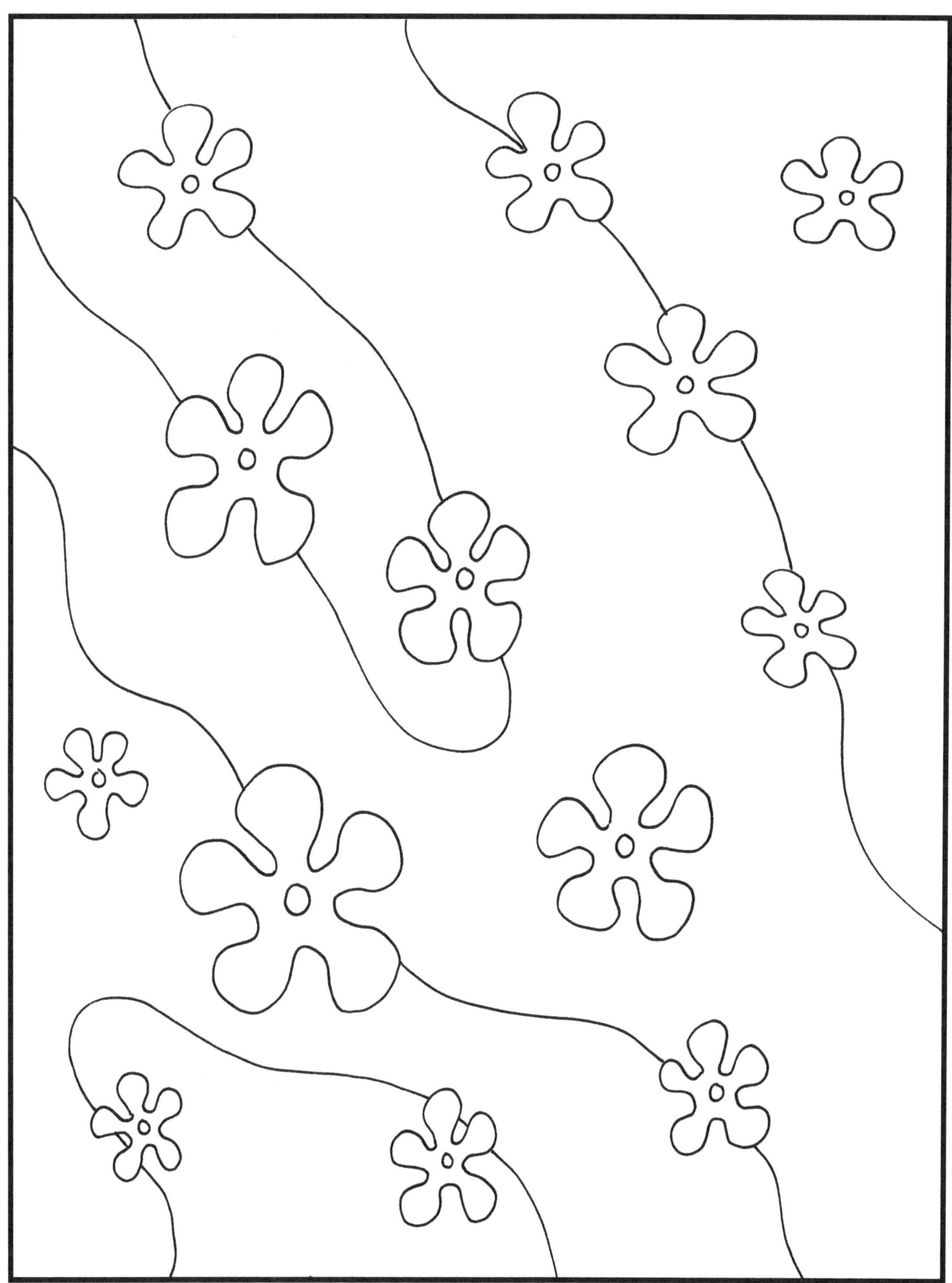

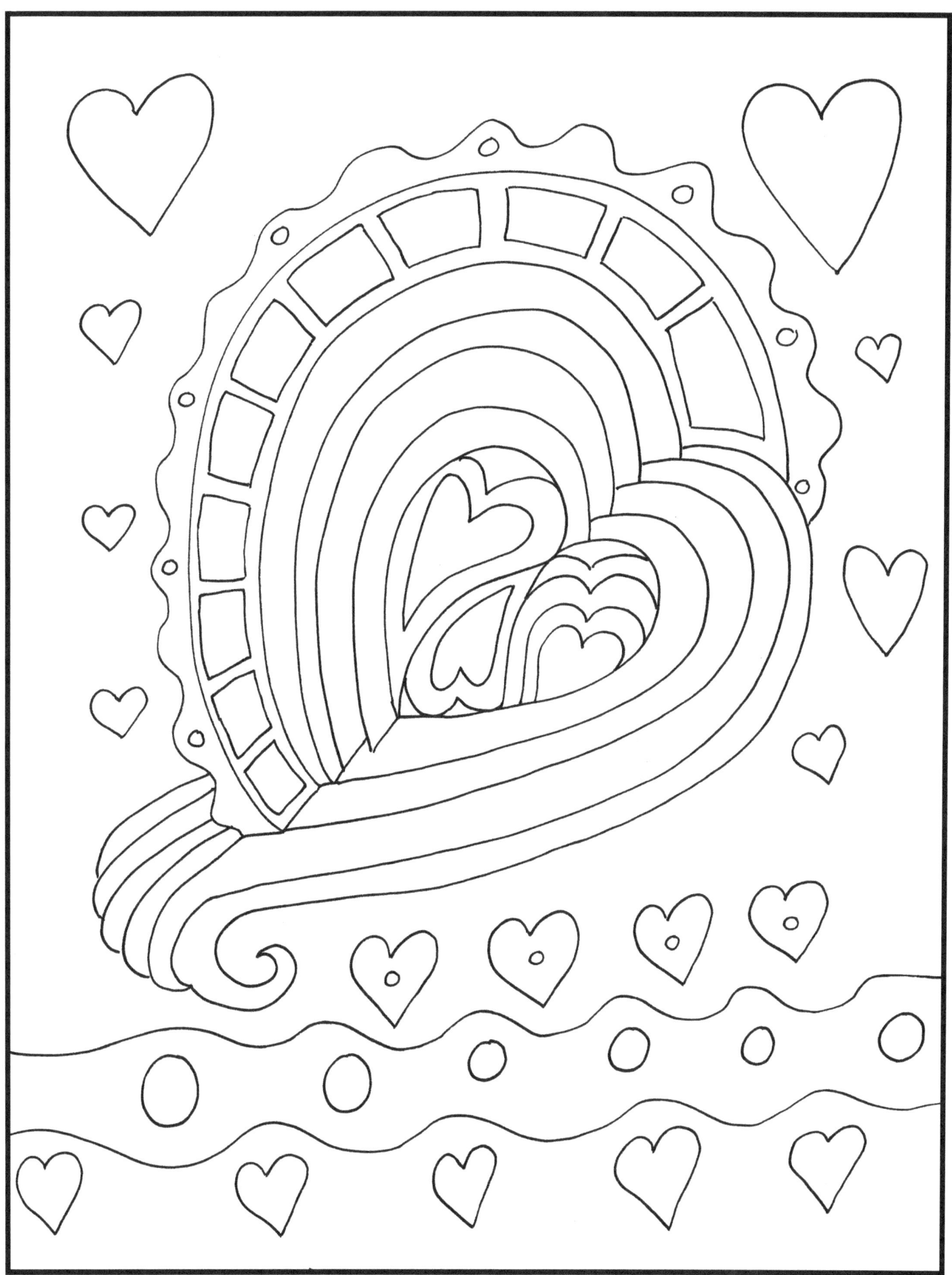

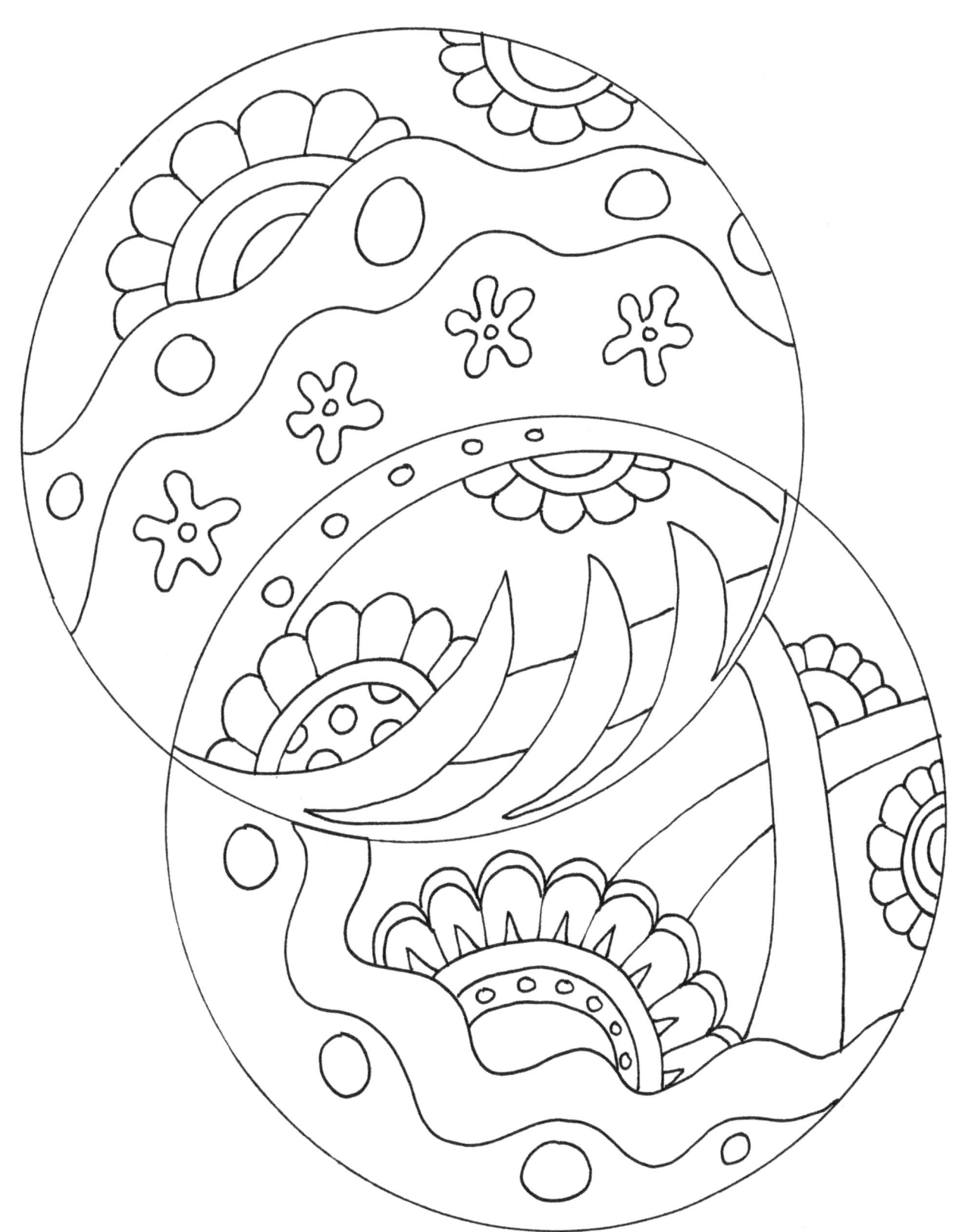

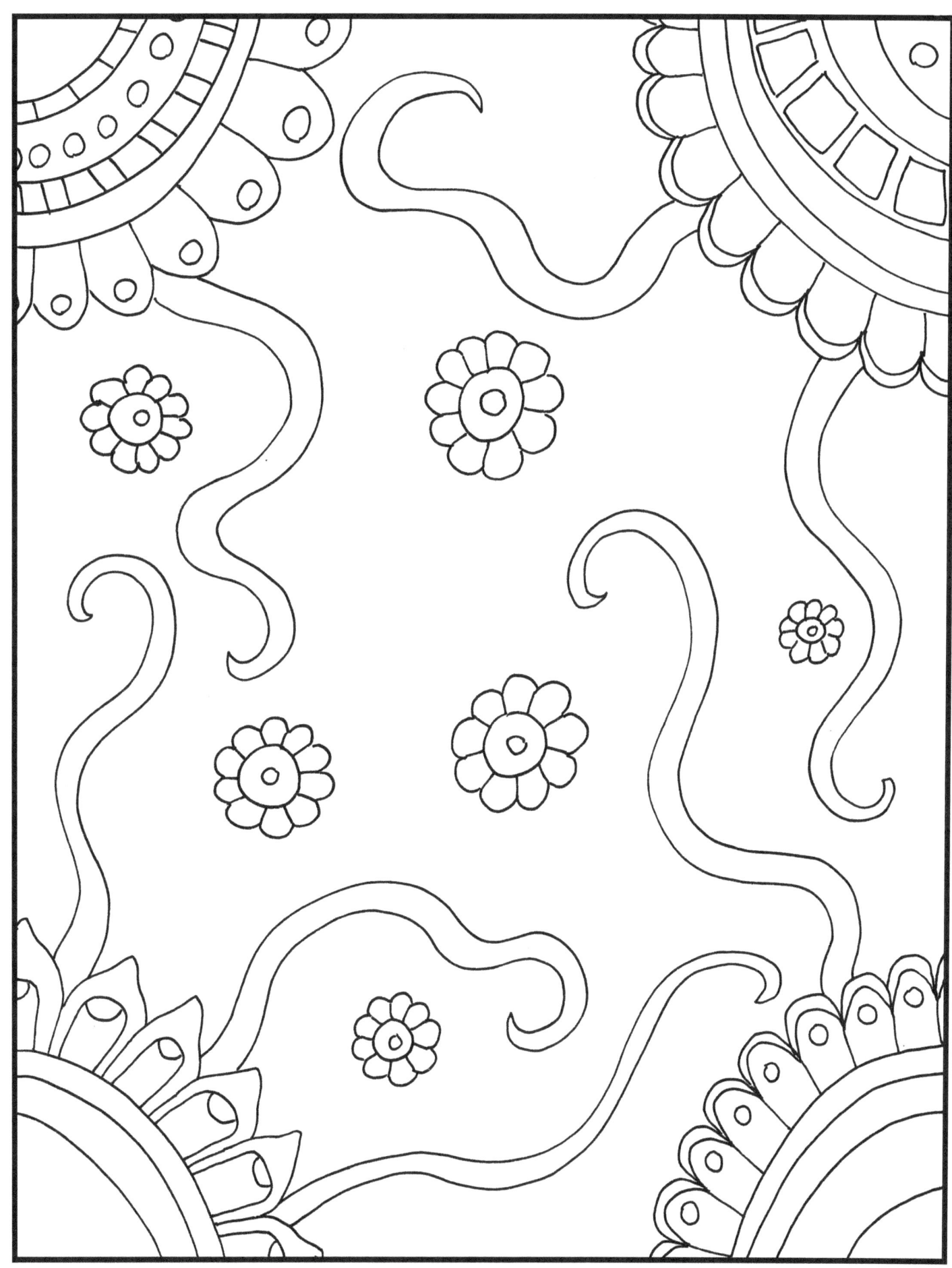

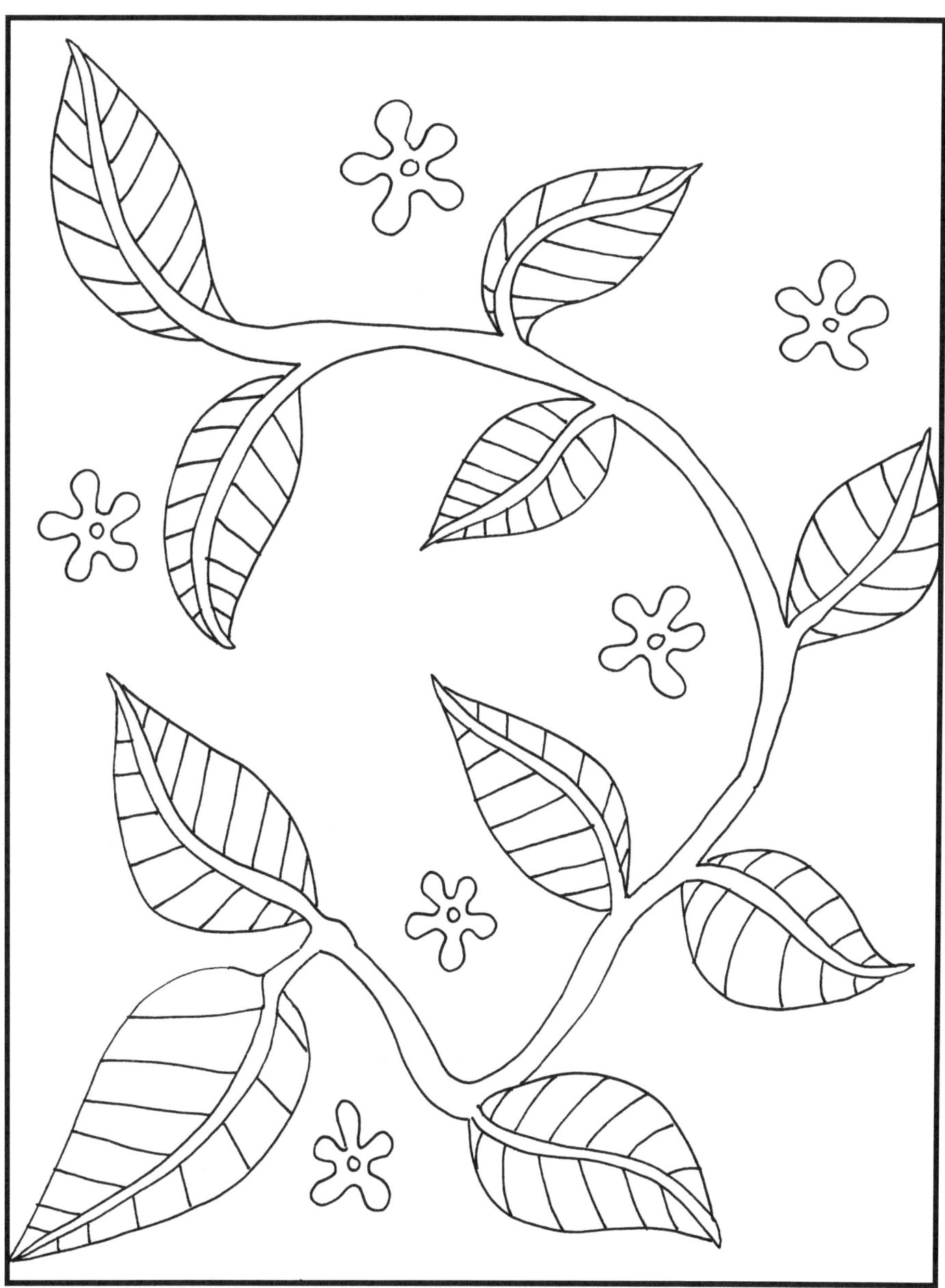

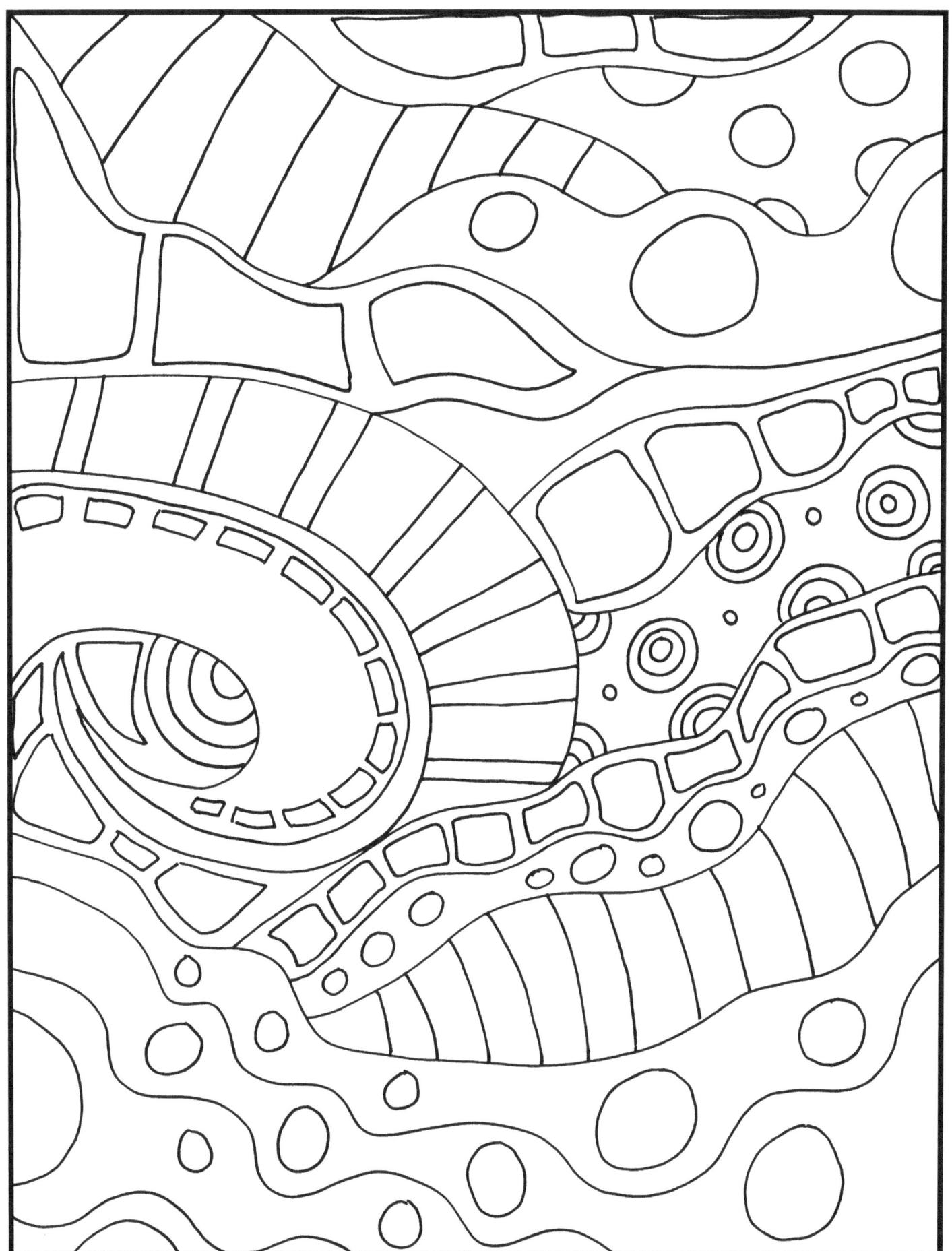

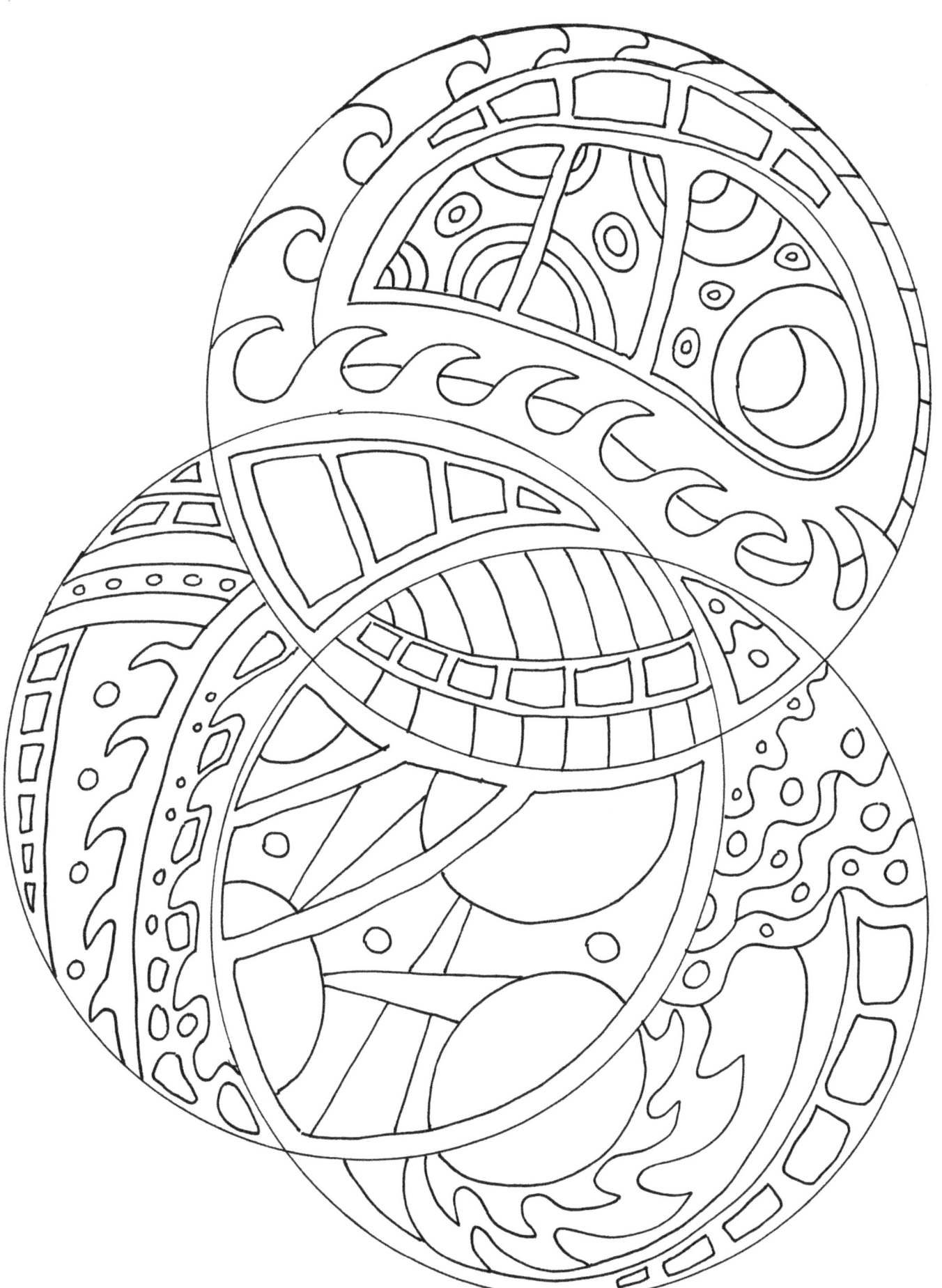

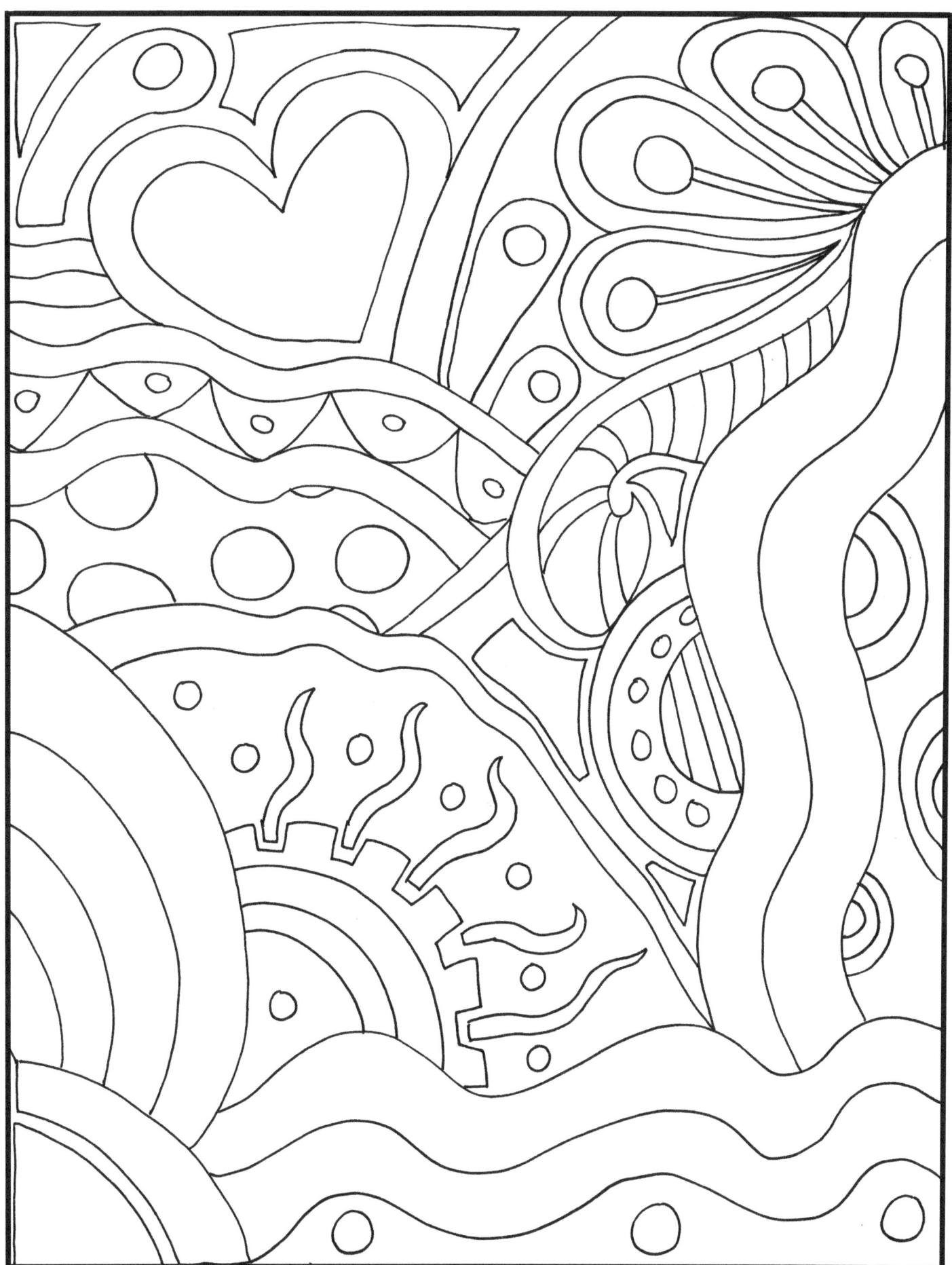

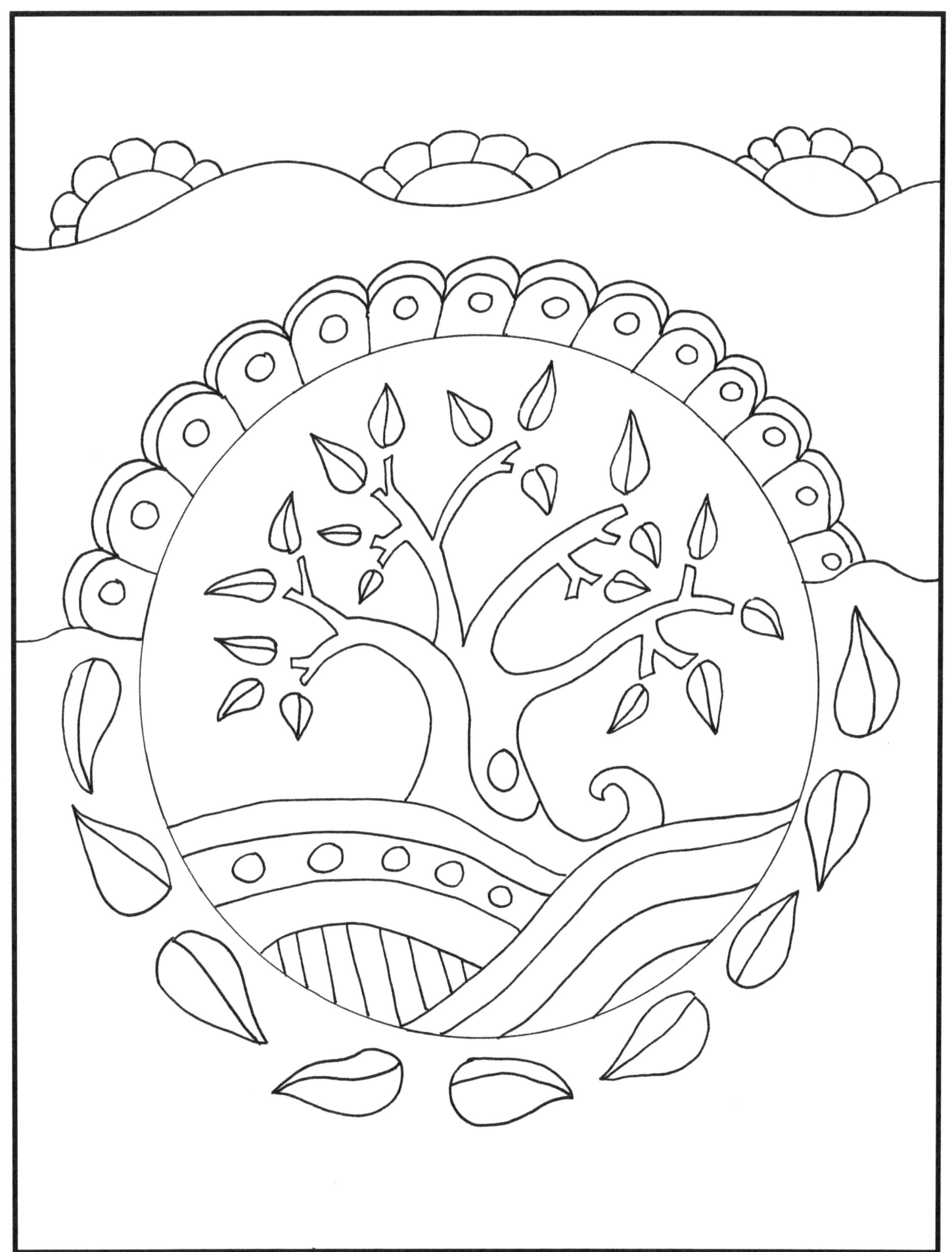

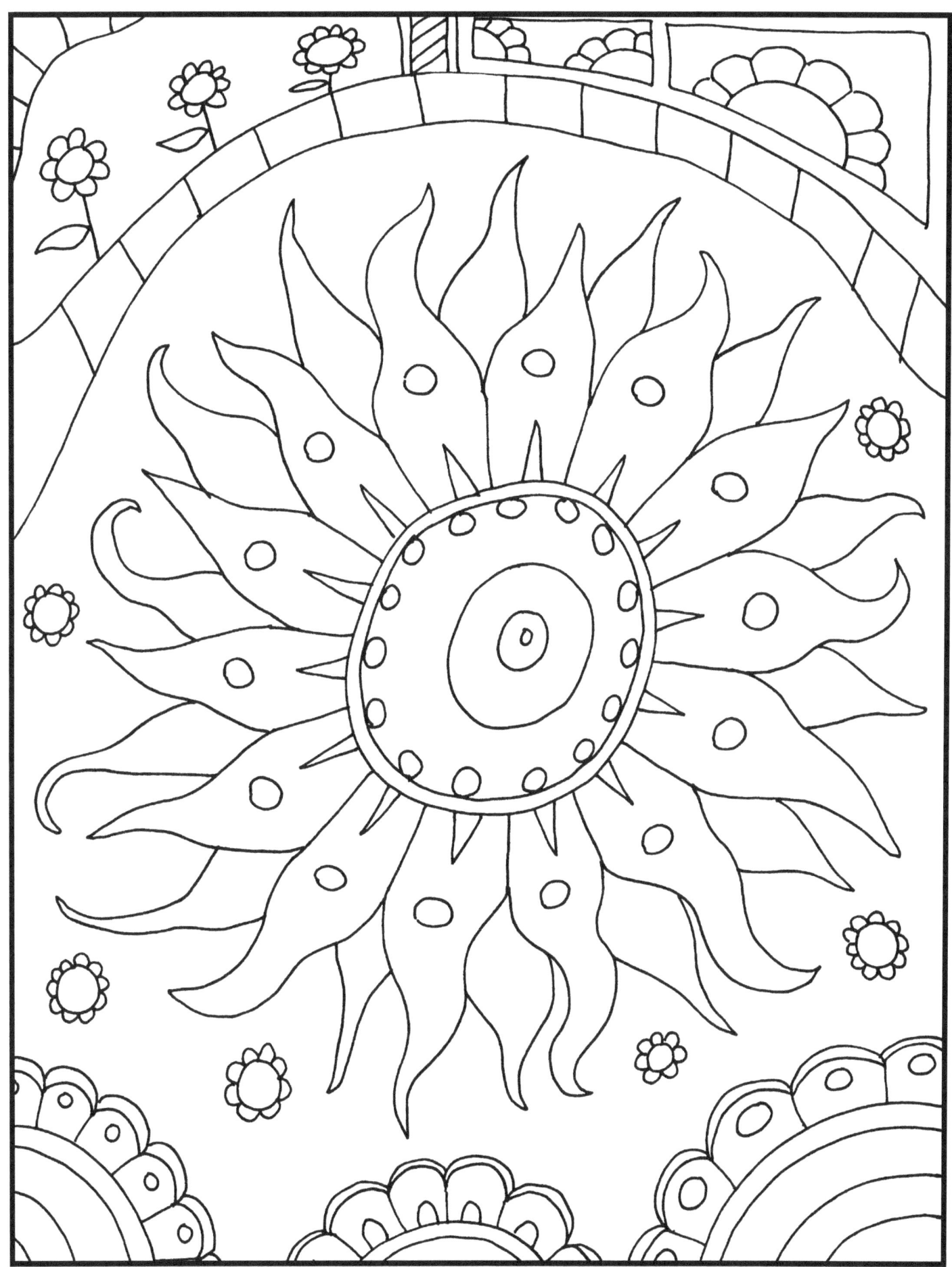

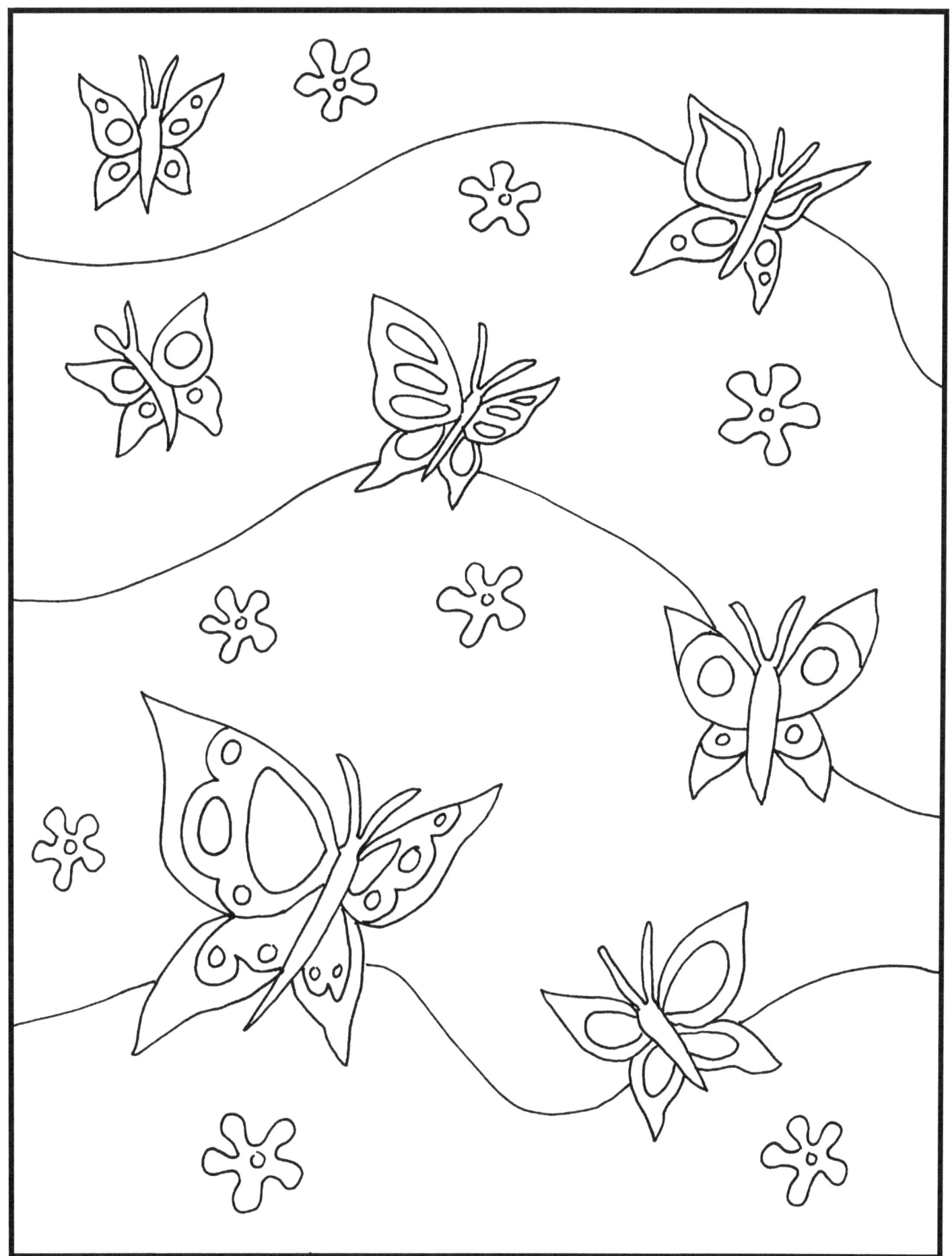

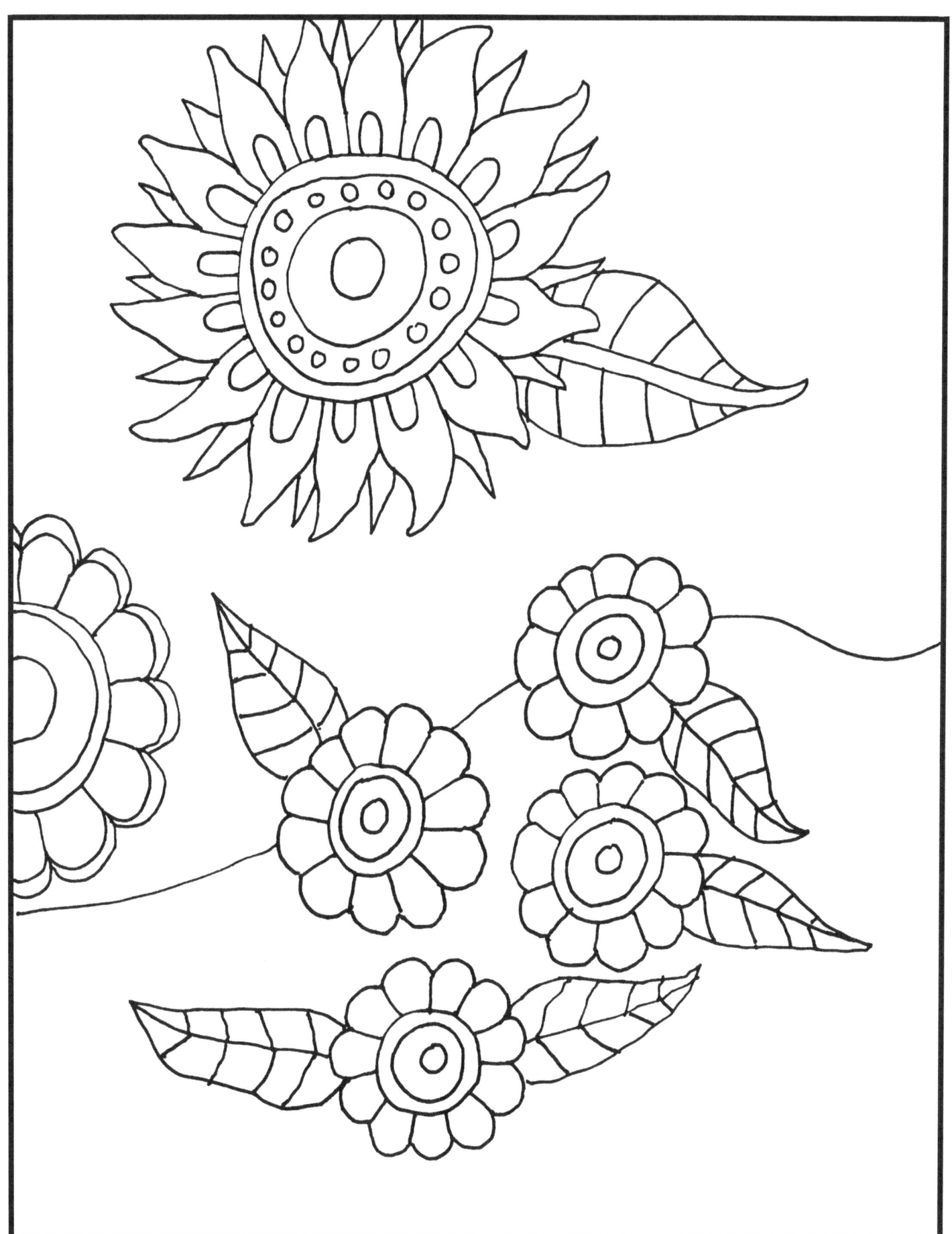

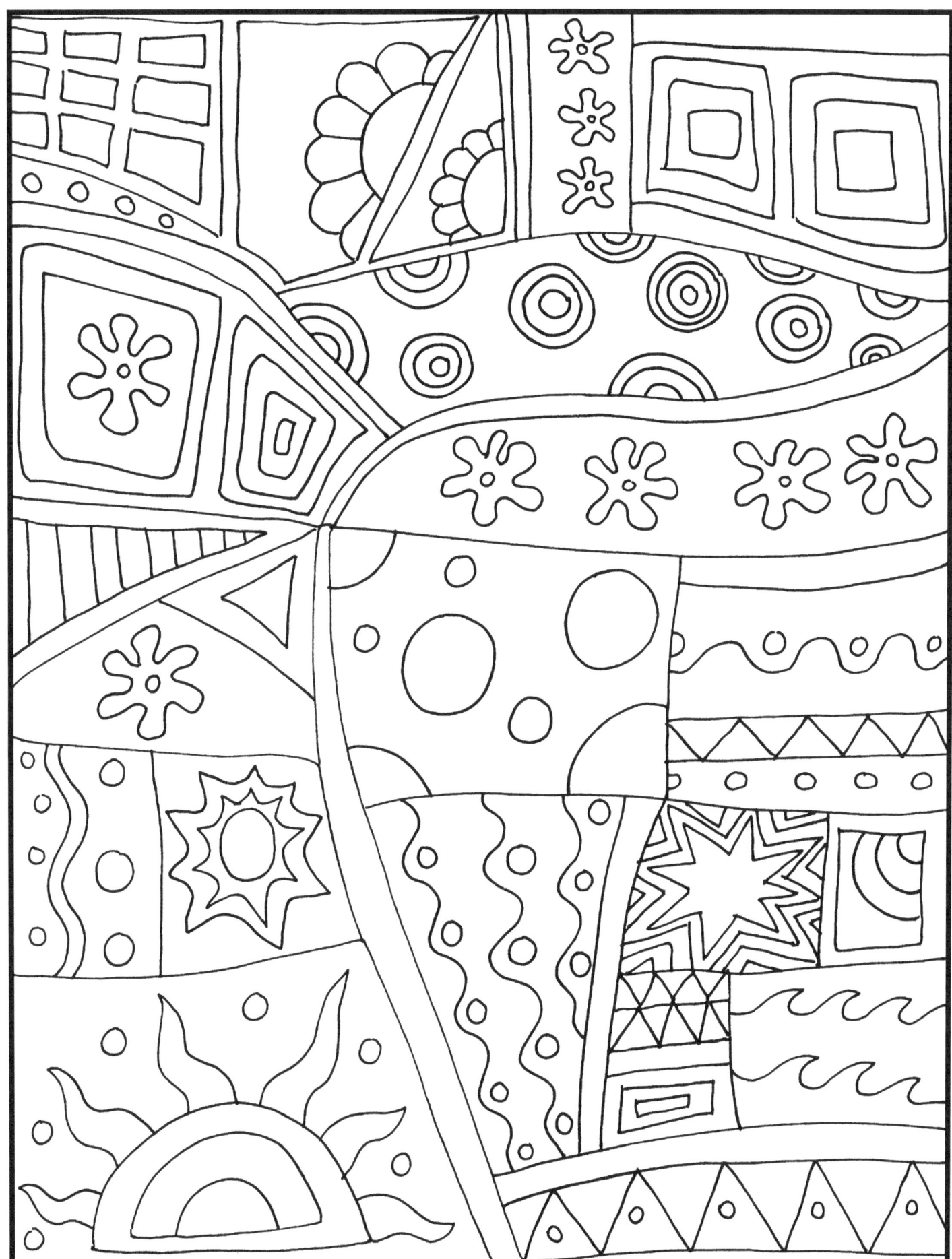

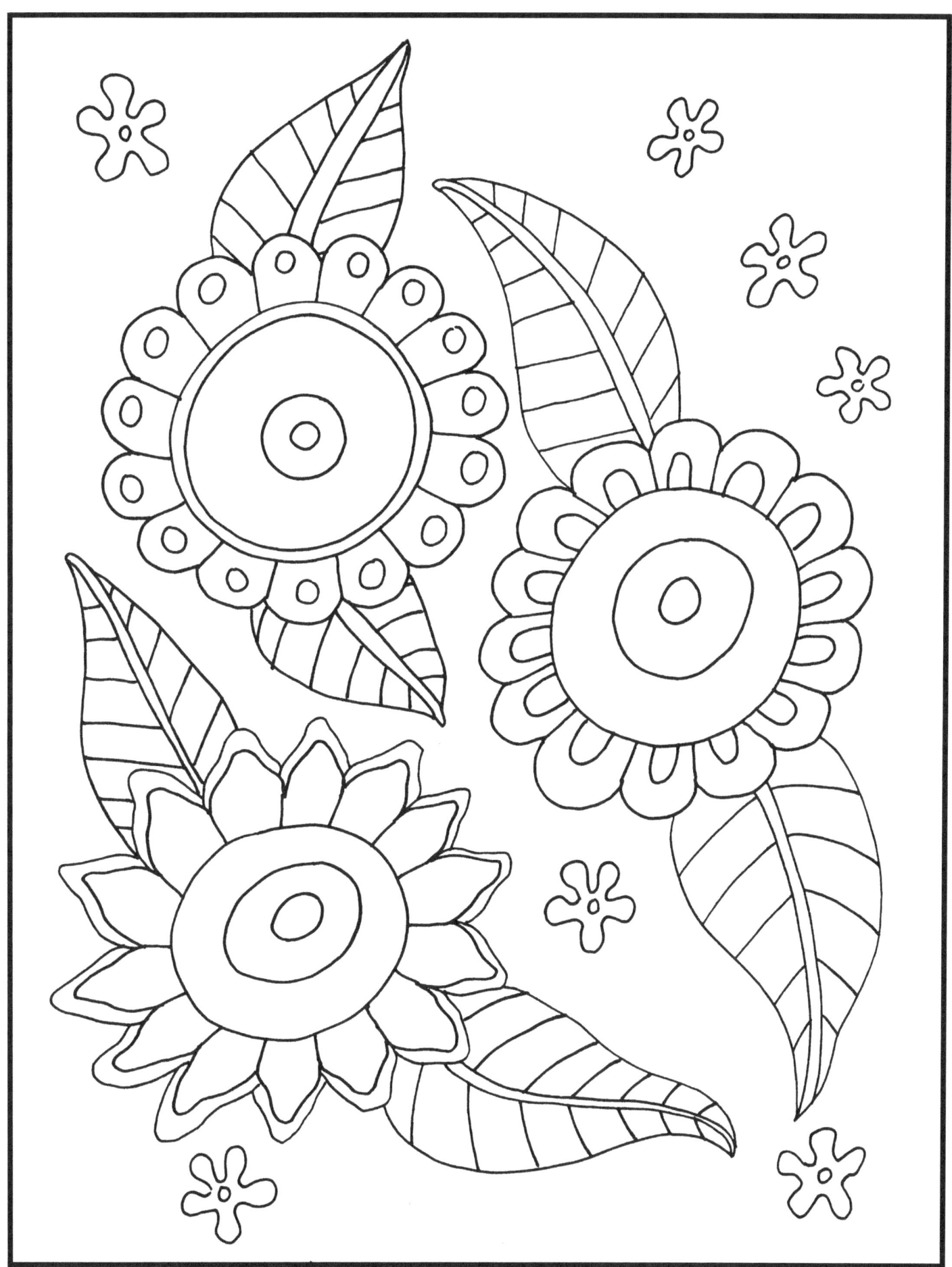

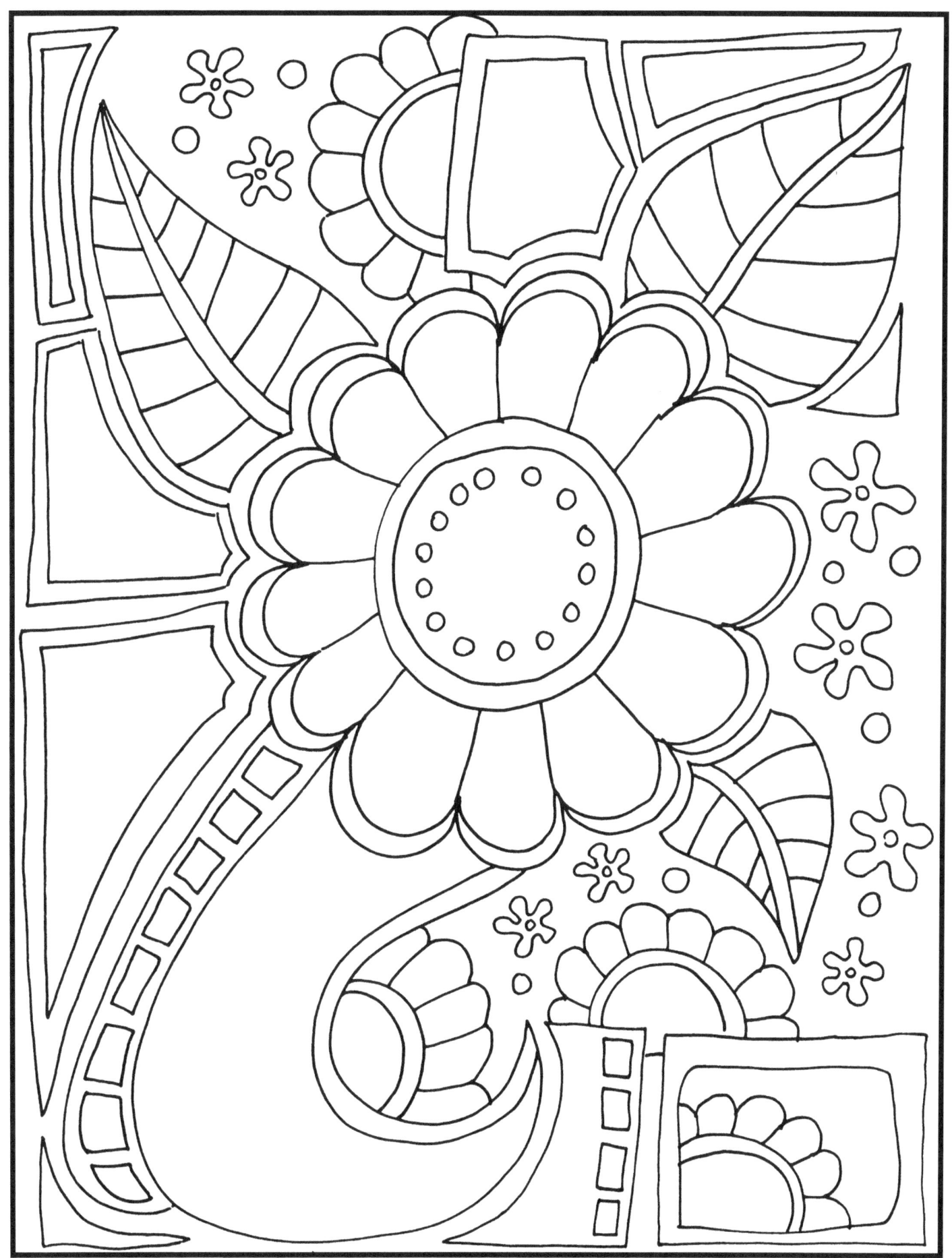

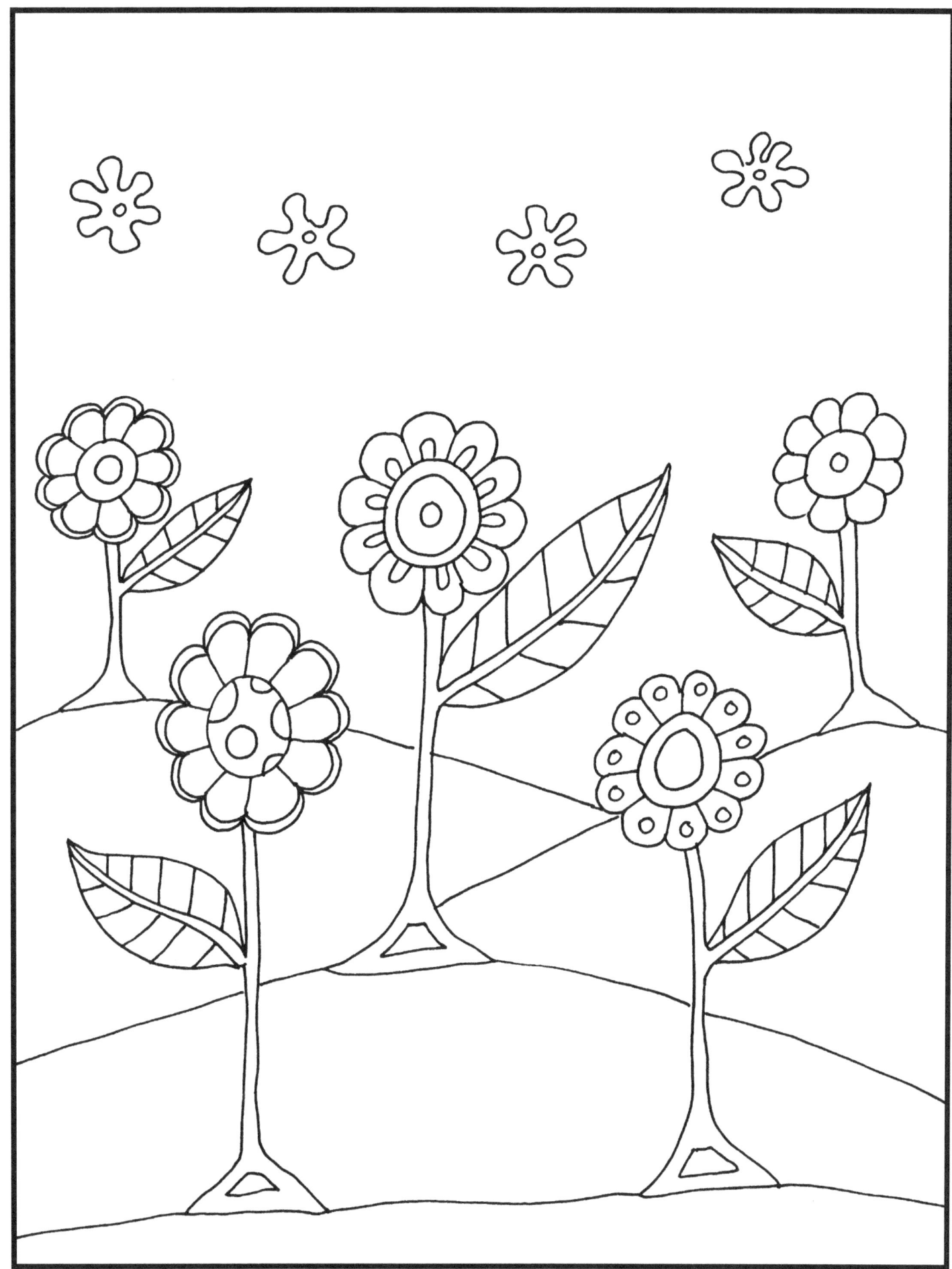

Also available by Kimberly Garvey:

- **Strange Designs** - An adult coloring book for everyone.

- **Strange Little Designs** - A mini/ travel adult coloring book.

- **Simple Designs** - An adult coloring book with easier pages.

- **It's Complicated** - A challenging. more detailed coloring book for the daring colorists.

PROTECTION PAGE

Kimberlygarvey.com

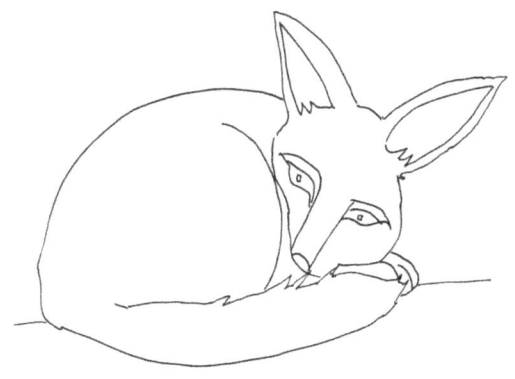